Country Casseroles

Country Casseroles

p. 4

p. 52

p. 68

Breakfast & Brunch

Egg & Sausage Casserole

½ pound pork sausage
3 tablespoons margarine or butter, divided
2 tablespoons all-purpose flour
¼ teaspoon salt
¼ teaspoon black pepper
1¼ cups milk

2 cups frozen hash brown potatoes
4 eggs, hard boiled and thinly sliced
½ cup cornflake crumbs
¼ cup sliced green onions
Fresh dill and oregano sprigs and chives (optional)

PREHEAT oven to 350¡F. Spray 2-quart oval casserole with nonstick cooking spray. Crumble sausage into large skillet; brown over medium-high heat until no longer pink, stirring to separate sausage. Drain sausage on paper towels. Discard fat and wipe skillet with paper towel.

MELT 2 tablespoons margarine in same skillet over medium heat. Stir in flour, salt and pepper until smooth. Gradually stir in milk; cook and stir until thickened. Add sausage, potatoes and eggs; stir to combine. Pour into prepared dish. Melt remaining 1 tablespoon margarine. Combine cornflake crumbs and melted margarine in small bowl; sprinkle evenly over sausage mixture.

BAKE, uncovered, 30 minutes or until hot and bubbly. Sprinkle with green onions. Garnish, if desired. *Makes 6 servings*

Mexican Roll-Ups with Avocado Sauce

8 eggs
2 tablespoons milk
1 tablespoon margarine or
    butter
1½ cups (6 ounces) shredded
    Monterey Jack cheese
1 large tomato, seeded and
    chopped
¼ cup chopped fresh
    cilantro
8 (6-inch) corn or flour
    tortillas

1½ cups salsa
2 medium avocados,
    chopped
¼ cup reduced-calorie sour
    cream
2 tablespoons diced green
    chilies
1 tablespoon fresh lemon
    juice
1 teaspoon hot pepper
    sauce
¼ teaspoon salt

PREHEAT oven to 350°F. Spray 13×9-inch baking dish with
nonstick cooking spray.

WHISK eggs and milk in medium bowl until blended. Melt margarine
in large skillet over medium heat; add egg mixture to skillet. Cook
and stir 5 minutes or until eggs are set, but still soft. Remove from
heat. Stir in cheese, tomato and cilantro.

SPOON about ⅓ cup egg mixture evenly down center of each
tortilla. Roll up tortillas and place seam side down in prepared dish.
Pour salsa evenly over tortillas. Cover tightly with foil and bake
20 minutes or until heated through.

Meanwhile, **PROCESS** avocados, sour cream, chilies, lemon juice,
hot pepper sauce and salt in food processor or blender until smooth.
Serve roll-ups with avocado sauce.   *Makes 8 servings*

Cook's Nook

To reduce fat, omit avocado sauce
and serve with additional salsa and nonfat
sour cream.

Breakfast Pizza

1 can (10 ounces) refrigerated biscuit dough
½ pound bacon slices
2 tablespoons margarine or butter
2 tablespoons all-purpose flour

¼ teaspoon salt
⅛ teaspoon black pepper
1½ cups milk
½ cup (2 ounces) shredded sharp Cheddar cheese
¼ cup sliced green onions
¼ cup chopped red bell pepper

PREHEAT oven to 350°F. Spray 13×9-inch baking dish with nonstick cooking spray.

SEPARATE biscuit dough and arrange side by side in rectangle on lightly floured surface without overlapping. Roll into 14×10-inch rectangle. Place in prepared dish; pat edges up sides of dish. Bake 15 minutes. Remove from oven and set aside.

Meanwhile, **PLACE** bacon in single layer in large skillet; cook over medium heat until crisp. Remove from skillet; drain on paper towels. Crumble and set aside.

MELT margarine in medium saucepan over medium heat. Stir in flour, salt and black pepper until smooth. Gradually stir in milk; cook and stir until thickened. Stir in cheese until melted. Spread sauce evenly over baked crust. Sprinkle bacon, green onions and bell pepper over sauce.

BAKE, uncovered, 20 minutes or until crust is golden brown.

Makes 6 servings

Chili Cheese Puff

¾ **cup all-purpose flour**
1½ **teaspoons baking powder**
9 **eggs**
4 **cups (16 ounces)**
   shredded Monterey
   Jack cheese
2 **cups (1 pint) 1% milkfat**
   cottage cheese

2 **cans (4 ounces each)**
   diced green chilies,
   drained
1½ **teaspoons sugar**
¼ **teaspoon salt**
⅛ **teaspoon hot pepper**
   sauce
1 **cup salsa**

PREHEAT oven to 350°F. Spray 13×9-inch baking dish with nonstick cooking spray.

COMBINE flour and baking powder in small bowl.

WHISK eggs in large bowl until blended; add Monterey Jack cheese, cottage cheese, chilies, sugar, salt and hot pepper sauce. Add flour mixture; stir just until combined. Pour into prepared dish.

BAKE, uncovered, 45 minutes or until egg mixture is set. Let stand 5 minutes before serving. Serve with salsa.   *Makes 8 servings*

Cook's Nook

For a spicy addition, substitute a jalapeño pepper for the diced green chilies. Seed and dice the jalapeño and add to egg mixture. Be careful when handling pepper because it can sting and irritate the skin. Wash hands after handling.

Menu

Chili Cheese Puff

Sausage Patties

Mango or Papaya Slices

Assorted Muffins

Orange Juice

Apple & Raisin Oven Pancake

1 large baking apple, cored
   and thinly sliced
⅓ cup golden raisins
2 tablespoons packed
   brown sugar
½ teaspoon ground
   cinnamon
4 eggs

⅔ cup milk
⅔ cup all-purpose flour
2 tablespoons margarine or
   butter, melted
Powdered sugar
   (optional)
Raspberries and fresh
   mint (optional)

PREHEAT oven to 350°F. Spray 9-inch pie plate with nonstick cooking spray.

COMBINE apple, raisins, brown sugar and cinnamon in medium bowl. Transfer to prepared pie plate.

BAKE, uncovered, 10 to 15 minutes or until apple begins to soften. Remove from oven. *Increase oven temperature to 450°F.*

Meanwhile, **WHISK** eggs, milk, flour and margarine in medium bowl until blended. Pour batter over apple mixture.

BAKE 15 minutes or until pancake is golden brown. Sprinkle with powdered sugar, if desired. Garnish with raspberries and mint, if desired. *Makes 6 servings*

Cook's Nook

Apple varieties best for baking are Cortland, Northern Spy, Rome Beauty, Winesap and York Imperial.

French Toast Strata

4 ounces day-old French or
  Italian bread, cut into
  ¾-inch cubes (4 cups)
⅓ cup golden raisins
1 package (3 ounces)
  cream cheese, cut into
  ¼-inch cubes
3 eggs
1½ cups milk

½ cup maple-flavored
  pancake syrup
1 teaspoon vanilla
2 tablespoons sugar
1 teaspoon ground
  cinnamon
Additional maple-flavored
  pancake syrup
  (optional)

SPRAY 11×7-inch baking dish with nonstick cooking spray. Place bread cubes in even layer in prepared dish; sprinkle raisins and cream cheese evenly over bread.

BEAT eggs in medium bowl with electric mixer at medium speed until blended. Add milk, ½ cup pancake syrup and vanilla; mix well. Pour egg mixture evenly over bread mixture. Cover; refrigerate at least 4 hours or overnight.

PREHEAT oven to 350°F. Combine sugar and cinnamon in small bowl; sprinkle evenly over bread mixture.

BAKE, uncovered, 40 to 45 minutes or until puffy, golden brown and knife inserted in center comes out clean. Cut into squares and serve with additional pancake syrup, if desired. *Makes 6 servings*

Beef & Pork

Chili Spaghetti Casserole

8 ounces uncooked
   spaghetti
1 pound lean ground beef
1 medium onion, chopped
¼ teaspoon salt
⅛ teaspoon black pepper
1 can (15 ounces)
   vegetarian chili with
   beans
1 can (14½ ounces) Italian-
   style stewed tomatoes,
   undrained

1½ cups (6 ounces) shredded
   sharp Cheddar cheese,
   divided
½ cup reduced-fat sour
   cream
1½ teaspoons chili powder
¼ teaspoon garlic powder

PREHEAT oven to 350°F. Spray 13×9-inch baking dish with nonstick cooking spray.

COOK pasta according to package directions until al dente. Drain and place in prepared dish.

Meanwhile, **PLACE** beef and onion in large skillet; sprinkle with salt and pepper. Brown beef over medium-high heat until beef is no longer pink, stirring to separate beef. Drain fat from skillet. Stir in chili, tomatoes with juice, 1 cup cheese, sour cream, chili powder and garlic powder.

ADD chili mixture to pasta; stir until pasta is well coated. Sprinkle with remaining ½ cup cheese.

COVER tightly with foil and bake 30 minutes or until hot and bubbly. Let stand 5 minutes before serving. *Makes 8 servings*

Ham, Barley and Almond Bake

....

½ cup slivered almonds
1 tablespoon margarine or
  butter
1 cup uncooked barley
1 cup chopped carrots
1 bunch green onions,
  sliced
2 ribs celery, sliced
3 cloves garlic, minced
1 pound lean smoked ham,
  cubed
2 teaspoons dried basil
  leaves

1 teaspoon dried oregano
  leaves
¼ teaspoon black pepper
2 cans (14 ounces each)
  reduced-sodium beef
  broth
½ pound fresh green beans,
  cut into 1-inch pieces
Fresh basil leaves and
  carrot ribbons
  (optional)

PREHEAT oven to 350°F. Spray 13×9-inch baking dish with nonstick cooking spray.

SPREAD almonds in single layer on baking sheet. Bake 5 minutes or until golden brown, stirring frequently.

MELT margarine in large skillet over medium-high heat. Add barley, chopped carrots, onions, celery and garlic; cook and stir 2 minutes or until onions are tender. Remove from heat. Stir in ham, toasted almonds, dried basil, oregano and pepper. Pour into prepared dish.

POUR broth into medium saucepan; bring to a boil over high heat. Pour over barley mixture.

COVER tightly with foil and bake 20 minutes. Remove from oven; stir in green beans. Bake, covered, 30 minutes or until barley is tender. Garnish with fresh basil and carrot ribbons, if desired.

Makes 8 servings

Hearty Biscuit-Topped Steak Pie

1½ pounds top round steak, cooked and cut into 1-inch cubes

1 package (9 ounces) frozen baby carrots

1 package (9 ounces) frozen peas and pearl onions

1 large baking potato, cooked, peeled and cut into ½-inch pieces

1 jar (18 ounces) home-style brown gravy

½ teaspoon dried thyme leaves

½ teaspoon black pepper

1 can (12 ounces) refrigerated flaky buttermilk biscuits

PREHEAT oven to 375°F. Spray 11×7-inch baking dish with nonstick cooking spray.

COMBINE steak, frozen vegetables and potato in prepared dish. Stir in gravy, thyme and pepper.

BAKE, uncovered, 40 minutes. Remove from oven. *Increase oven temperature to 400°F.* Top with biscuits and bake 8 to 10 minutes or until biscuits are golden brown.   *Makes 6 servings*

Cook's Nook

This casserole can be prepared with leftovers of almost any kind. Other steaks, roast beef, stew meat, pork, lamb or chicken can be substituted for round steak; adjust gravy flavor to complement meat. Red potatoes can be used in place of baking potato. Choose your favorite vegetable combination as a substitute for the peas, onions and carrots.

Family-Style Hot Dogs with Red Beans and Rice

1 tablespoon vegetable oil
1 medium onion, chopped
½ medium green bell
　 pepper, chopped
2 cloves garlic, minced
1 can (14 ounces) kidney
　 beans, drained and
　 rinsed
1 can (14 ounces) Great
　 Northern beans,
　 drained and rinsed

½ pound beef hot dogs, cut
　 into ¼-inch-thick slices
1 cup uncooked instant
　 brown rice
1 cup vegetable broth
¼ cup ketchup
¼ cup packed brown sugar
3 tablespoons dark
　 molasses
1 tablespoon Dijon mustard
　 Zucchini ribbons (optional)

PREHEAT oven to 350°F. Spray 13×9-inch baking dish with nonstick cooking spray.

HEAT oil in Dutch oven over medium-high heat until hot. Add onion, pepper and garlic; cook and stir 2 minutes or until onion is tender.

ADD beans, hot dogs, rice, broth, ketchup, sugar, molasses and mustard to vegetables; stir to combine. Pour into prepared dish.

COVER tightly with foil and bake 30 minutes or until rice is tender. Garnish with zucchini, if desired. _Makes 6 servings_

Smoked sausage can be substituted for hot dogs. Cut sausage into ¼-inch-thick slices and add with beans.

Beefy Nacho Crescent Bake

1 pound lean ground beef
½ cup chopped onion
¼ teaspoon salt
⅛ teaspoon black pepper
1 tablespoon chili powder
1 teaspoon ground cumin
1 teaspoon dried oregano
  leaves
1 can (11 ounces)
  condensed nacho
  cheese soup, undiluted

1 cup milk
1 can (8 ounces)
  refrigerated crescent
  roll dough
¼ cup (1 ounce) shredded
  Cheddar cheese
Chopped fresh cilantro
  (optional)
Salsa (optional)

PREHEAT oven to 375°F. Spray 13×9-inch baking dish with nonstick cooking spray.

PLACE beef and onion in large skillet; sprinkle with salt and pepper. Brown beef over medium-high heat until no longer pink, stirring to separate beef. Drain fat. Stir in chili powder, cumin and oregano. Cook and stir 2 minutes; remove from heat.

COMBINE soup and milk in medium bowl, stirring until smooth. Pour soup mixture into prepared dish, spreading evenly.

SEPARATE crescent dough into 4 rectangles; press perforations together firmly. Roll out each rectangle to 8×4 inches. Cut each rectangle in half crosswise to form 8 (4-inch) squares.

SPOON about ¼ cup beef mixture in center of each square. Lift 4 corners of dough up over filling to meet in center; pinch and twist firmly to seal. Place squares in dish.

BAKE, uncovered, 20 to 25 minutes or until crusts are golden brown. Sprinkle cheese over squares. Bake 5 minutes or until cheese melts. To serve, spoon soup mixture over each serving; sprinkle with cilantro, if desired. Serve with salsa, if desired.

Makes 4 servings

Reuben Noodle Bake

8 ounces uncooked egg
   noodles
5 ounces thinly sliced
   corned beef
1 can (14½ ounces)
   sauerkraut with
   caraway seeds, drained
2 cups (8 ounces) shredded
   Swiss cheese
½ cup Thousand Island
   dressing

½ cup milk
1 tablespoon prepared
   mustard
2 slices pumpernickel
   bread
1 tablespoon margarine or
   butter, melted
Red onion slices
   (optional)

PREHEAT oven to 350°F. Spray 13×9-inch baking dish with nonstick cooking spray.

COOK noodles according to package directions until al dente. Drain and set aside.

Meanwhile, **CUT** corned beef into bite-size pieces. Combine noodles, corned beef, sauerkraut and cheese in large bowl. Pour into prepared dish.

COMBINE dressing, milk and mustard in small bowl. Spoon dressing mixture evenly over noodle mixture.

TEAR bread into large pieces. Process in food processor or blender until crumbs are formed. Combine bread crumbs and margarine in small bowl; sprinkle evenly over casserole.

BAKE, uncovered, 25 to 30 minutes or until heated through. Garnish with red onion, if desired.   *Makes 6 servings*

Serving Suggestion: Serve with a mixed green salad.

Spicy Manicotti

3 cups ricotta cheese
1 cup grated Parmesan
   cheese, divided
2 eggs, lightly beaten
2½ tablespoons chopped
   fresh parsley
1 teaspoon dried Italian
   seasoning
½ teaspoon garlic powder
½ teaspoon salt
½ teaspoon black pepper

1 pound spicy Italian
   sausage, casing
   removed
1 can (28 ounces) crushed
   tomatoes in purée,
   undrained
1 jar (26 ounces) marinara
   or spaghetti sauce
8 ounces uncooked
   manicotti noodles

PREHEAT oven to 375°F. Spray 13×9-inch baking dish with nonstick cooking spray.

COMBINE ricotta cheese, ¾ cup Parmesan cheese, eggs, parsley, Italian seasoning, garlic powder, salt and pepper in medium bowl; set aside.

CRUMBLE sausage into large skillet; brown over medium-high heat until no longer pink, stirring to separate sausage. Drain sausage on paper towels; drain fat from skillet.

ADD tomatoes with juice and marinara sauce to same skillet; bring to a boil over high heat. Reduce heat to low; simmer, uncovered, 10 minutes. Pour about one third of sauce into prepared dish.

STUFF each uncooked noodle with about ½ cup cheese mixture. Place in dish. Top noodles with sausage; pour remaining sauce over noodles.

COVER tightly with foil and bake 50 minutes to 1 hour or until noodles are tender. Let stand 5 minutes before serving. Serve with remaining ¼ cup Parmesan cheese.   *Makes 8 servings*

Menu

Spicy Manicotti

Tossed Salad with
Vinaigrette Dressing

Garlic Bread

Italian Ice

Coffee

Pork Chops and Apple Stuffing

6 (¾-inch-thick) boneless
  pork loin chops (about
  1½ pounds)
¼ teaspoon salt
⅛ teaspoon black pepper
1 tablespoon vegetable oil
1 small onion, chopped
2 ribs celery, chopped
2 Granny Smith apples,
  peeled, cored and
  coarsely chopped
  (about 2 cups)

1 can (14½ ounces)
  reduced-sodium
  chicken broth
1 can (10¾ ounces)
  condensed cream of
  celery soup, undiluted
¼ cup dry white wine
6 cups herb-seasoned
  stuffing cubes

PREHEAT oven to 375°F. Spray 13×9-inch baking dish with
nonstick cooking spray.

SPRINKLE both sides of pork chops with salt and pepper. Heat oil
in large deep skillet over medium-high heat until hot. Add pork chops
and cook until browned on both sides, turning once. Remove from
skillet; set aside.

ADD onion and celery to same skillet. Cook and stir 3 minutes or
until onion is tender. Add apples; cook and stir 1 minute. Add broth,
soup and wine; stir until smooth. Bring to a simmer; remove from
heat. Stir in stuffing cubes until evenly moistened.

POUR stuffing mixture into prepared dish, spreading evenly. Place
pork chops on top of stuffing; pour any accumulated juices over pork
chops.

COVER tightly with foil and bake 30 to 40 minutes or until pork
chops are juicy and barely pink in centers.   *Makes 6 servings*

Serving Suggestion: Serve with a mixed green salad.

Beef Stroganoff Casserole

1 pound lean ground beef
¼ teaspoon salt
⅛ teaspoon black pepper
1 teaspoon vegetable oil
8 ounces sliced
    mushrooms
1 large onion, chopped
3 cloves garlic, minced
¼ cup dry white wine
1 can (10¾ ounces)
    condensed cream of
    mushroom soup,
    undiluted

½ cup sour cream
1 tablespoon Dijon mustard
4 cups cooked egg noodles
    Chopped fresh parsley
    (optional)
    Radish slices and fresh
    Italian parsley sprigs
    (optional)

PREHEAT oven to 350°F. Spray 13×9-inch baking dish with nonstick cooking spray.

PLACE beef in large skillet; sprinkle with salt and pepper. Brown beef over medium-high heat until no longer pink, stirring to separate beef. Drain fat from skillet; set aside beef.

HEAT oil in same skillet over medium-high heat until hot. Add mushrooms, onion and garlic; cook and stir 2 minutes or until onion is tender. Add wine. Reduce heat to medium-low and simmer 3 minutes. Remove from heat; stir in soup, sour cream and mustard until well combined. Return beef to skillet.

PLACE noodles in prepared dish. Pour beef mixture over noodles; stir until well coated.

BAKE, uncovered, 30 minutes or until heated through. Sprinkle with chopped parsley, if desired. Garnish with radish and parsley sprigs, if desired.
                                        Makes 6 servings

Chicken & Turkey

Turkey & Green Bean Casserole

¼ cup slivered almonds
1 package (7 ounces) herb-seasoned stuffing cubes
¾ cup reduced-sodium chicken broth
1 can (10¾ ounces) condensed cream of mushroom soup, undiluted
¼ cup milk or half-and-half

¼ teaspoon black pepper
1 package (10 ounces) frozen French-style green beans, thawed and drained
2 cups diced cooked turkey or chicken (about ¾ pound)
Red bell pepper slices and fresh Italian parsley (optional)

PREHEAT oven to 350°F. Spray 11×7-inch baking dish with nonstick cooking spray. Spread almonds in single layer on baking sheet. Bake 5 minutes or until golden brown, stirring frequently. Set aside.

ADD stuffing to prepared dish; drizzle with broth. Stir to coat stuffing with broth. Combine soup, milk and black pepper in large bowl; stir in green beans and turkey. Spoon over stuffing; top with almonds.

BAKE, uncovered, 30 to 35 minutes or until heated through. Garnish with bell pepper and Italian parsley, if desired.   *Makes 4 servings*

Tip: Buying sliced turkey from the deli counter at your supermarket is a great way to save time when preparing a casserole. Just dice the turkey and add it to the casserole.

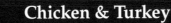

Coq au Vin

½ cup all-purpose flour
1¼ teaspoons salt
¾ teaspoon black pepper
3½ pounds chicken pieces
2 tablespoons margarine or
   butter
8 ounces mushrooms, cut
   in half if large
4 cloves garlic, minced
¾ cup chicken broth

¾ cup dry red wine
2 teaspoons dried thyme
   leaves
1½ pounds red potatoes,
   quartered
2 cups frozen pearl onions
   (about 8 ounces)
   Chopped fresh parsley
   (optional)

PREHEAT oven to 350°F.

COMBINE flour, salt and pepper in large resealable plastic food storage bag. Add chicken, two pieces at a time, and seal bag. Shake to coat chicken; remove chicken and set aside. Repeat with remaining pieces. Reserve remaining flour mixture.

MELT margarine in ovenproof Dutch oven over medium-high heat. Arrange chicken in single layer in Dutch oven and cook 3 minutes per side or until browned. Transfer to plate; set aside. Repeat with remaining pieces.

ADD mushrooms and garlic to Dutch oven; cook and stir 2 minutes. Sprinkle reserved flour mixture over mushroom mixture; cook and stir 1 minute. Add broth, wine and thyme; bring to a boil over high heat, stirring to scrape browned bits from bottom of Dutch oven. Add potatoes and onions; return to a boil. Remove from heat and place chicken in Dutch oven, partially covering chicken with broth mixture.

BAKE, covered, about 45 minutes or until chicken is no longer pink in centers, juices run clear and sauce is slightly thickened. Transfer chicken and vegetables to shallow bowls. Spoon sauce over chicken and vegetables. Sprinkle with parsley, if desired.

Makes 4 to 6 servings

Serving Suggestion: Serve with assorted fresh baked rolls.

Chicken Tetrazzini

8 ounces uncooked vermicelli, broken in half

1 can (10¾ ounces) condensed cream of mushroom soup, undiluted

¼ cup half-and-half

3 tablespoons dry sherry

½ teaspoon salt

⅛ to ¼ teaspoon crushed red pepper flakes

2 cups diced cooked chicken (about ¾ pound)

1 cup frozen peas

½ cup grated Parmesan cheese

1 cup fresh coarse bread crumbs

2 tablespoons margarine or butter, melted

Chopped fresh basil (optional)

Lemon slices and lettuce leaves (optional)

PREHEAT oven to 375°F. Spray 13×9-inch baking dish with nonstick cooking spray.

COOK pasta according to package directions until al dente. Drain and set aside.

Meanwhile, **COMBINE** soup, half-and-half, sherry, salt and pepper flakes in large bowl. Stir in chicken, peas and cheese. Add pasta to chicken mixture; stir until pasta is coated. Pour into prepared dish.

COMBINE bread crumbs and margarine in small bowl. Sprinkle evenly over casserole.

BAKE, uncovered, 25 to 30 minutes or until heated through and bread crumbs are golden brown. Sprinkle with basil, if desired. Garnish with lemon and lettuce, if desired.   *Makes 4 servings*

Turkey Meatball & Olive Casserole

2 cups uncooked rotini
    pasta
½ pound ground turkey
¼ cup dry bread crumbs
1 egg, slightly beaten
2 teaspoons dried minced
    onion
2 teaspoons white wine
    Worcestershire sauce
½ teaspoon dried Italian
    seasoning
½ teaspoon salt
⅛ teaspoon black pepper

1 tablespoon vegetable oil
1 can (10¾ ounces)
    condensed cream of
    celery soup, undiluted
½ cup low-fat plain yogurt
¾ cup pimiento-stuffed
    green olives, sliced
3 tablespoons Italian-style
    bread crumbs
1 tablespoon margarine or
    butter, melted
Paprika (optional)
Fresh herbs (optional)

PREHEAT oven to 350°F. Spray 2-quart round casserole with nonstick cooking spray.

COOK pasta according to package directions until al dente. Drain and set aside.

Meanwhile, **COMBINE** turkey, ¼ cup bread crumbs, egg, onion, Worcestershire, Italian seasoning, salt and pepper in medium bowl. Shape mixture into 1-inch meatballs.

HEAT oil in medium skillet over high heat until hot. Add meatballs in single layer; cook until lightly browned on all sides and still pink in centers, turning frequently. *Do not overcook.* Remove from skillet; drain on paper towels.

MIX soup and yogurt in large bowl. Add pasta, meatballs and olives; stir gently to combine. Transfer to prepared dish.

COMBINE 3 tablespoons bread crumbs and margarine in small bowl; sprinkle evenly over casserole. Sprinkle lightly with paprika, if desired.

BAKE, covered, 30 minutes. Uncover and bake 12 minutes or until meatballs are no longer pink in centers and casserole is hot and bubbly. Garnish with herbs, if desired.   *Makes 6 to 8 servings*

Chicken Pot Pie

2 tablespoons margarine or
    butter
¾ pound boneless skinless
    chicken breasts, cut
    into 1-inch pieces
¾ teaspoon salt
8 ounces fresh green
    beans, cut into 1-inch
    pieces (about 2 cups)
½ cup chopped red bell
    pepper
½ cup thinly sliced celery

3 tablespoons all-purpose
    flour
½ cup chicken broth
½ cup half-and-half
1 teaspoon dried thyme
    leaves
½ teaspoon rubbed sage
1 cup frozen pearl onions
½ cup frozen corn
    Pastry for single-crust
    10-inch pie

PREHEAT oven to 425°F. Spray 10-inch deep-dish pie plate with
nonstick cooking spray.

MELT margarine in large deep skillet over medium-high heat. Add
chicken; cook and stir 3 minutes or until no longer pink in centers.
Sprinkle with salt. Add green beans, pepper and celery; cook and stir
3 minutes.

SPRINKLE flour evenly over chicken and vegetables; cook and stir
1 minute. Stir in broth, half-and-half, thyme and sage; bring to a boil
over high heat. Reduce heat to low and simmer 3 minutes or until
sauce is thickened. Stir in onions and corn. Return to a simmer; cook
and stir 1 minute.

TRANSFER mixture to prepared pie plate. Place pie pastry over
chicken mixture; turn pastry edge under and flute to seal. Cut 4 slits
in pie pastry to allow steam to escape.

BAKE, uncovered, 20 minutes or until crust is light golden brown
and chicken mixture is hot and bubbly. Let stand 5 minutes before
serving.   *Makes 6 servings*

Indian-Spiced Chicken with Wild Rice

½ teaspoon salt
½ teaspoon ground cumin
½ teaspoon black pepper
¼ teaspoon ground
    cinnamon
¼ teaspoon ground
    turmeric
4 boneless skinless
    chicken breast halves
    (about 1 pound)
2 tablespoons olive oil
2 carrots, sliced

1 red bell pepper, chopped
1 rib celery, chopped
2 cloves garlic, minced
1 package (6 ounces) long
    grain and wild rice mix
2 cups reduced-sodium
    chicken broth
1 cup raisins
¼ cup sliced almonds
    Red bell pepper slices
    (optional)

COMBINE salt, cumin, black pepper, cinnamon and turmeric in small bowl. Rub spice mixture on both sides of chicken. Place chicken on plate; cover and refrigerate 30 minutes.

PREHEAT oven to 350°F. Spray 9-inch square baking dish with nonstick cooking spray.

HEAT oil in large skillet over medium-high heat until hot. Add chicken; cook 2 minutes per side or until browned. Transfer to clean plate; set aside.

PLACE carrots, chopped bell pepper, celery and garlic in same skillet. Cook and stir 2 minutes. Add rice; cook 5 minutes, stirring frequently. Add broth and seasoning packet from rice mix; bring to a boil over high heat. Remove from heat; stir in raisins. Pour into prepared dish; place chicken on rice mixture. Sprinkle with almonds.

COVER tightly with foil and bake 35 minutes or until chicken is no longer pink in centers, juices run clear and rice is tender. Garnish with bell pepper slices, if desired.   *Makes 4 servings*

Southern-Style Chicken and Greens

1 teaspoon salt
1 teaspoon paprika
½ teaspoon black pepper
3½ pounds chicken pieces
4 thick slices smoked
    bacon (4 ounces), cut
    crosswise into ¼-inch
    pieces
1 cup uncooked rice

2 cups packed coarsely
    chopped fresh collard
    or mustard greens or
    kale (3 to 4 ounces)
1 can (14½ ounces) stewed
    tomatoes, undrained
1¼ cups chicken broth
    Tomato wedges and
    fresh Italian parsley
    (optional)

PREHEAT oven to 350°F.

COMBINE salt, paprika and pepper in small bowl. Sprinkle top of chicken pieces with salt mixture; set aside.

PLACE bacon in ovenproof Dutch oven; cook over medium heat until crisp. Drain on paper towels. Reserve bacon fat. Heat bacon fat over medium-high heat until hot. Arrange chicken in single layer in Dutch oven and cook 3 minutes per side or until browned. Transfer to clean plate; set aside. Repeat with remaining pieces. Reserve 1 tablespoon bacon fat in Dutch oven; discard remaining bacon fat.

ADD rice to Dutch oven; cook and stir 1 minute. Add collard greens, tomatoes with juice, broth and half of bacon; bring to a boil over high heat. Remove from heat; arrange chicken over rice mixture.

BAKE, covered, about 40 minutes or until chicken is no longer pink in centers, juices run clear and most of liquid is absorbed. Let stand 5 minutes before serving. Transfer to serving platter; sprinkle with remaining bacon. Garnish with tomato and Italian parsley, if desired.

Makes 4 to 6 servings

Menu

Southern-Style Chicken and Greens

Corn Bread

Peach Cobbler with Vanilla Ice Cream

Iced Tea and Lemonade

Chicken Marsala

6 ounces uncooked broad
    egg noodles
½ cup Italian-style dry
    bread crumbs
1 teaspoon dried basil
    leaves
1 egg
1 teaspoon water
4 boneless skinless
    chicken breast halves
3 tablespoons olive oil,
    divided
¾ cup chopped onion

8 ounces cremini or button
    mushrooms, sliced
3 cloves garlic, minced
3 tablespoons all-purpose
    flour
1 can (14½ ounces)
    chicken broth
½ cup dry marsala wine
¾ teaspoon salt
¼ teaspoon black pepper
    Chopped fresh parsley
    (optional)

PREHEAT oven to 375°F. Spray 11×7-inch baking dish with nonstick cooking spray. Cook noodles according to package directions until al dente. Drain and place in prepared dish.

Meanwhile, **COMBINE** bread crumbs and basil on shallow plate or pie plate. Beat egg with water on another shallow plate or pie plate. Dip chicken in egg mixture, letting excess drip off. Roll in crumb mixture, patting to coat. Heat 2 tablespoons oil in large skillet over medium-high heat until hot. Cook chicken 3 minutes per side or until browned. Transfer to clean plate; set aside.

HEAT remaining 1 tablespoon oil in same skillet over medium heat. Add onion; cook and stir 5 minutes. Add mushrooms and garlic; cook and stir 3 minutes. Sprinkle flour over onion mixture; cook and stir 1 minute. Add broth, wine, salt and pepper; bring to a boil over high heat. Cook and stir 5 minutes or until sauce thickens. Reserve ½ cup sauce. Pour remaining sauce over noodles; stir until noodles are well coated. Place chicken on top of noodles. Spoon reserved sauce over chicken.

BAKE, uncovered, 20 minutes or until chicken is no longer pink in centers. Sprinkle with parsley, if desired.   *Makes 4 servings*

Turkey and Biscuits

2 cans (10¾ ounces each)
   condensed cream of
   chicken soup, undiluted
¼ cup dry white wine
¼ teaspoon poultry
   seasoning
2 packages (8 ounces each)
   frozen cut asparagus,
   thawed

3 cups diced cooked turkey
   or chicken
Paprika (optional)
1 can (11 ounces)
   refrigerated flaky
   biscuits

PREHEAT oven to 350°F. Spray 13×9-inch baking dish with nonstick cooking spray.

COMBINE soup, wine and poultry seasoning in medium bowl.

ARRANGE asparagus in single layer in prepared dish. Place turkey evenly over asparagus. Spread soup mixture over turkey. Sprinkle lightly with paprika, if desired.

COVER tightly with foil and bake 20 minutes. Remove from oven. *Increase oven temperature to 425°F.* Top with biscuits and bake, uncovered, 8 to 10 minutes or until biscuits are golden brown.

Makes 6 servings

Poultry seasoning is a powdered herb blend of sage, thyme, marjoram, savory, onion, black pepper and celery seed.

Artichoke-Olive Chicken Bake

1½ cups uncooked rotini pasta
1 tablespoon olive oil
1 medium onion, chopped
½ green bell pepper, chopped
2 cups shredded cooked chicken
1 can (14½ ounces) diced tomatoes with Italian-style herbs, undrained

1 can (14 ounces) artichoke hearts, drained and quartered
1 can (6 ounces) sliced black olives, drained
1 teaspoon dried Italian seasoning
2 cups (8 ounces) shredded mozzarella cheese
Fresh basil sprig (optional)

PREHEAT oven to 350°F. Spray 13×9-inch baking dish with nonstick cooking spray.

COOK pasta according to package directions until al dente. Drain and set aside.

Meanwhile, **HEAT** oil in large deep skillet over medium heat until hot. Add onion and pepper; cook and stir 1 minute. Add chicken, tomatoes with juice, pasta, artichokes, olives and Italian seasoning; mix until combined.

PLACE half of chicken mixture in prepared dish; sprinkle with half of cheese. Top with remaining chicken mixture and cheese.

BAKE, covered, 35 minutes or until hot and bubbly. Garnish with basil, if desired.   *Makes 8 servings*

Cook's Nook

Serve with crusty Italian or French bread and a tossed salad.

Roasted Chicken and Vegetables over Wild Rice

....

3½ pounds chicken pieces
  ¾ cup olive oil vinaigrette
      dressing, divided
  1 tablespoon margarine or
      butter, melted
  1 package (6 ounces) long
      grain and wild rice mix
  1 can (13¾ ounces)
      reduced-sodium
      chicken broth
  1 small eggplant, cut into
      1-inch pieces
  2 medium red potatoes, cut
      into 1-inch pieces

1 medium yellow squash,
    cut into 1-inch pieces
1 medium zucchini, cut into
    1-inch pieces
1 medium red onion, cut
    into wedges
1 package (4 ounces)
    crumbled feta cheese
    with basil
  Chopped fresh cilantro
    (optional)
  Fresh thyme sprig
    (optional)

REMOVE skin from chicken; discard. Combine chicken and ½ cup dressing in large resealable plastic food storage bag. Seal bag and turn to coat. Refrigerate 30 minutes or overnight.

PREHEAT oven to 375°F. Coat bottom of 13×9-inch baking dish with margarine.

ADD rice and seasoning packet to prepared dish; stir in broth. Combine eggplant, potatoes, squash, zucchini and onion in large bowl. Place on top of rice mixture.

REMOVE chicken from bag and place on top of vegetables; discard marinade. Pour remaining ¼ cup dressing over chicken.

BAKE, uncovered, 45 minutes. Remove from oven and sprinkle with cheese. Bake 5 to 10 minutes or until chicken is no longer pink in centers, juices run clear and cheese is melted. Sprinkle with cilantro, if desired. Garnish with thyme, if desired.   *Makes 4 to 6 servings*

Fish & Shellfish

Flounder Fillets over Zesty Lemon Rice

¼ cup margarine or butter
3 tablespoons fresh lemon
    juice
2 teaspoons chicken
    bouillon granules
½ teaspoon black pepper
1 cup cooked rice
1 package (10 ounces)
    frozen chopped
    broccoli, thawed

1 cup (4 ounces) shredded
    sharp Cheddar cheese
1 pound flounder fillets
½ teaspoon paprika
    Lemon slices, lemon peel
    and fresh parsley
    (optional)

PREHEAT oven to 375°F. Spray 2-quart square casserole with nonstick cooking spray.

MELT margarine in small saucepan over medium heat. Add lemon juice, bouillon and pepper; cook and stir 2 minutes or until bouillon is dissolved.

COMBINE rice, broccoli, cheese and ¼ cup lemon sauce in medium bowl; spread on bottom of prepared dish. Place fillets on top of rice mixture. Pour remaining lemon sauce over fillets.

BAKE, uncovered, 20 minutes or until fish flakes easily when tested with fork. Sprinkle evenly with paprika. Garnish with lemon and parsley, if desired.   *Makes 6 servings*

Tuna Noodle Casserole

....

8 ounces uncooked elbow macaroni

2 tablespoons margarine or butter

¾ cup chopped onion

½ cup thinly sliced celery

½ cup finely chopped red bell pepper

2 tablespoons all-purpose flour

1 teaspoon salt

⅛ teaspoon ground white pepper

1½ cups milk

1 can (6 ounces) albacore tuna in water, drained

½ cup grated Parmesan cheese, divided

Fresh dill sprigs (optional)

PREHEAT oven to 375°F. Spray 8-inch square baking dish with nonstick cooking spray.

COOK pasta according to package directions until al dente. Drain and set aside.

Meanwhile, **MELT** margarine in large deep skillet over medium heat. Add onion; cook and stir 3 minutes. Add celery and bell pepper; cook and stir 3 minutes. Sprinkle flour, salt and white pepper over vegetables; cook and stir 1 minute. Gradually stir in milk; cook and stir until thickened. Remove from heat.

ADD pasta, tuna and ¼ cup cheese to skillet; stir until pasta is well coated. Pour tuna mixture into prepared dish; sprinkle evenly with remaining ¼ cup cheese.

BAKE, uncovered, 20 to 25 minutes or until hot and bubbly. Garnish with dill, if desired.   *Makes 4 servings*

Cook's Nook

Serve with spinach salad and warm biscuits.

Jambalaya

· ·

1 teaspoon vegetable oil
½ pound smoked deli ham,
    cubed
½ pound smoked sausage,
    cut into ¼-inch-thick
    slices
1 large onion, chopped
1 large green bell pepper,
    chopped (about
    1½ cups)
3 ribs celery, chopped
    (about 1 cup)
3 cloves garlic, minced
1 can (28 ounces) diced
    tomatoes, undrained

1 can (10½ ounces)
    chicken broth
1 cup uncooked rice
1 tablespoon
    Worcestershire sauce
1 teaspoon dried thyme
    leaves
1 teaspoon salt
½ teaspoon black pepper
¼ teaspoon ground red
    pepper
1 package (12 ounces)
    frozen ready-to-cook
    shrimp, thawed
Fresh chives (optional)

PREHEAT oven to 350°F. Spray 13×9-inch baking dish with nonstick cooking spray.

HEAT oil in large skillet over medium-high heat until hot. Add ham and sausage. Cook and stir 5 minutes or until sausage is lightly browned on both sides. Remove from skillet and place in prepared dish. Place onion, bell pepper, celery and garlic in same skillet; cook and stir 3 minutes. Add to sausage mixture.

COMBINE tomatoes with juice, broth, rice, Worcestershire, thyme, salt and black and red peppers in same skillet; bring to a boil over high heat. Reduce heat to low and simmer 3 minutes. Pour over sausage mixture and stir until combined.

COVER tightly with foil and bake 45 minutes or until rice is almost tender. Remove from oven; place shrimp on top of rice mixture. Bake, uncovered, 10 minutes or until shrimp are pink and opaque. Garnish with chives, if desired.   *Makes 8 servings*

Pasta with Salmon and Dill

6 ounces uncooked mafalda
 pasta
1 tablespoon olive oil
2 ribs celery, sliced
1 small red onion, chopped
1 can (10¾ ounces)
 condensed cream of
 celery soup, undiluted
¼ cup reduced-fat
 mayonnaise
¼ cup dry white wine

3 tablespoons chopped
 fresh parsley
1 teaspoon dried dill weed
1 can (7½ ounces) pink
 salmon, drained
½ cup dry bread crumbs
1 tablespoon margarine or
 butter, melted
Fresh dill sprigs and red
 onion slices (optional)

PREHEAT oven to 350°F. Spray 1-quart square baking dish with
nonstick cooking spray.

COOK pasta according to package directions until al dente. Drain
and set aside.

Meanwhile, **HEAT** oil in medium skillet over medium-high heat until
hot. Add celery and chopped onion; cook and stir 2 minutes or until
vegetables are tender. Set aside.

COMBINE soup, mayonnaise, wine, parsley and dill weed in large
bowl. Stir in pasta, vegetables and salmon until pasta is well coated.
Pour salmon mixture into prepared dish.

COMBINE bread crumbs and margarine in small bowl; sprinkle
evenly over casserole.

BAKE, uncovered, 25 minutes or until hot and bubbly. Garnish with
fresh dill and red onion slices, if desired. *Makes 4 servings*

*Mafalda pasta is a broad, flat noodle
with rippled edges that is similar to a small
lasagna noodle.*

Menu

Pasta with Salmon and Dill

Buttered Steamed Carrots

Focaccia Bread

White Wine

Tuna Pot Pie

1 tablespoon margarine or butter
1 small onion, chopped
1 can (10¾ ounces) condensed cream of potato soup, undiluted
¼ cup milk
½ teaspoon dried thyme leaves
¼ teaspoon salt
⅛ teaspoon black pepper
2 cans (6 ounces each) albacore tuna in water, drained

1 package (16 ounces) frozen vegetable medley (such as broccoli, green beans, pearl onions and red peppers), thawed
2 tablespoons chopped fresh parsley
1 can (8 ounces) refrigerated crescent roll dough

PREHEAT oven to 350°F. Spray 11×7-inch baking dish with nonstick cooking spray.

MELT margarine in large skillet over medium heat. Add onion; cook and stir 2 minutes or until onion is tender. Add soup, milk, thyme, salt and pepper; cook and stir 3 to 4 minutes or until thick and bubbly. Stir in tuna, vegetables and parsley. Pour mixture into prepared dish.

UNROLL crescent roll dough and separate into triangles. Place triangles over tuna mixture without overlapping dough.

BAKE, uncovered, 20 minutes or until triangles are golden brown. Let stand 5 minutes before serving.   *Makes 6 servings*

Cook's Nook

Create an exciting recipe by substituting a new vegetable medley for the one listed. Enjoy the results!

Creamy "Crab" Fettuccine

....

1 pound imitation crabmeat
   sticks
6 ounces uncooked
   fettuccine
3 tablespoons margarine
   or butter, divided
1 small onion, chopped
2 ribs celery, chopped
½ medium red bell pepper,
   chopped
2 cloves garlic, minced
1 cup reduced-fat sour
   cream

1 cup reduced-fat
   mayonnaise
1 cup (4 ounces) shredded
   sharp Cheddar cheese
2 tablespoons chopped
   fresh parsley
¼ teaspoon salt
⅛ teaspoon black pepper
½ cup cornflake crumbs
   Fresh chives (optional)

PREHEAT oven to 350°F. Spray 2-quart square baking dish with nonstick cooking spray.

CUT crabmeat into bite-size pieces; set aside.

COOK pasta according to package directions until al dente. Drain and set aside.

Meanwhile, **MELT** 1 tablespoon margarine in large skillet over medium-high heat. Add onion, celery, bell pepper and garlic; cook and stir 2 minutes or until vegetables are tender. Set aside.

COMBINE sour cream, mayonnaise, cheese, parsley, salt and black pepper in large bowl. Add crabmeat, pasta and vegetable mixture, stirring gently to combine. Pour into prepared dish.

MELT remaining 2 tablespoons margarine. Combine cornflake crumbs and margarine in small bowl; sprinkle evenly over casserole.

BAKE, uncovered, 30 minutes or until hot and bubbly. Garnish with chives, if desired.

Makes 6 servings

Vegetables & Sides

Mexican Tortilla Stack-Ups

1 tablespoon vegetable oil
½ cup chopped onion
1 can (15 ounces) black
    beans, drained and
    rinsed
1 can (14½ ounces)
    Mexican- or Italian-style
    diced tomatoes,
    undrained
1 cup frozen corn

1 envelope (1¼ ounces)
    taco seasoning mix
6 (6-inch) corn tortillas
2 cups (8 ounces) shredded
    Cheddar cheese with
    taco seasonings
1 cup water
    Sour cream (optional)
    Sliced black olives
    (optional)

PREHEAT oven to 350¡F. Spray 13×9-inch baking dish with nonstick cooking spray.

HEAT oil in large skillet over medium-high heat until hot. Add onion; cook and stir 3 minutes or until tender. Add beans, tomatoes with juice, corn and taco seasoning mix. Bring to a boil over high heat. Reduce heat to low and simmer 5 minutes.

PLACE 2 tortillas side by side in prepared dish. Top each tortilla with about ½ cup bean mixture. Sprinkle evenly with one third of cheese. Repeat layers twice, creating 2 tortilla stacks each 3 tortillas high.

POUR water along sides of tortillas.

COVER tightly with foil and bake 30 to 35 minutes or until heated through. Cut into wedges to serve. Serve with sour cream and olives, if desired.   *Makes 6 servings*

Easy Cheesy Lasagna

· ·

2 tablespoons olive oil

3 small zucchini, quartered lengthwise and thinly sliced crosswise

1 package (8 ounces) mushrooms, thinly sliced

1 medium onion, chopped

5 cloves garlic, minced

2 containers (15 ounces each) reduced-fat ricotta cheese

¼ cup grated Parmesan cheese

2 eggs

½ teaspoon dried Italian seasoning

¼ teaspoon garlic salt

⅛ teaspoon black pepper

1 can (28 ounces) crushed tomatoes in purée, undrained

1 jar (26 ounces) spaghetti sauce

1 package (16 ounces) lasagna noodles, uncooked

4 cups (16 ounces) shredded mozzarella cheese

PREHEAT oven to 375¡F. Spray 13×9-inch baking dish or lasagna pan with nonstick cooking spray. Heat oil in large skillet over medium heat until hot. Add zucchini, mushrooms, onion and garlic; cook and stir 5 minutes.

COMBINE ricotta cheese, Parmesan cheese, eggs, Italian seasoning, garlic salt and pepper in medium bowl. Combine tomatoes and spaghetti sauce in another medium bowl.

SPREAD about ³⁄₄ cup tomato mixture in prepared dish. Place layer of uncooked noodles over tomato mixture, overlapping noodles. Spread half of vegetable mixture over noodles; top with half of ricotta cheese mixture. Sprinkle 1 cup mozzarella cheese over ricotta cheese mixture. Top with second layer of noodles. Spread about 1 cup tomato mixture over noodles. Top with remaining vegetable and ricotta cheese mixtures. Sprinkle with 1 cup mozzarella cheese. Top with third layer of noodles. Spread remaining tomato mixture over noodles. Sprinkle with remaining 2 cups mozzarella cheese.

COVER tightly with foil and bake 1 hour or until noodles in center are soft. Uncover; bake 5 minutes or until cheese is melted. Cover and let stand 15 minutes before serving.   *Makes 10 to 12 servings*

Greek Spinach and Feta Pie

⅓ cup butter, melted and
    divided
2 eggs
1 package (10 ounces)
    frozen chopped
    spinach, thawed and
    squeezed dry
1 container (15 ounces)
    ricotta cheese

1 package (4 ounces)
    crumbled feta cheese
¾ teaspoon finely grated
    lemon peel
¼ teaspoon black pepper
⅛ teaspoon ground nutmeg
1 package (16 ounces)
    frozen phyllo dough,
    thawed

PREHEAT oven to 350¡F. Brush 13×9-inch baking dish lightly with butter.

BEAT eggs in medium bowl. Stir in spinach, ricotta cheese, feta cheese, lemon peel, pepper and nutmeg. Set aside.

CUT 8 sheets of phyllo dough in half crosswise, forming 16 rectangles about 13×8½ inches each. Cover dough with damp cloth or plastic wrap while assembling pie. Reserve remaining dough for another use.

PLACE 1 piece of dough in prepared dish; brush top lightly with butter. Top with another piece of dough and brush lightly with butter. Continue layering with 6 pieces of dough, brushing each piece lightly with butter. Spoon spinach mixture evenly over dough. Top spinach mixture with piece of dough; brush lightly with butter. Repeat layering with remaining 7 pieces of dough, brushing each piece lightly with butter.

BAKE, uncovered, 35 to 40 minutes or until golden brown.

Makes 6 servings

Serving Suggestion: Serve with cantaloupe slices and cherries.

Baked Tomato Risotto

2 medium zucchini
1 jar (28 ounces) spaghetti
　　sauce
1 can (14 ounces) chicken
　　broth
1 cup uncooked arborio
　　rice

1 can (4 ounces) sliced
　　mushrooms
2 cups (8 ounces) shredded
　　mozzarella cheese
Yellow bell pepper slices
　　(optional)

PREHEAT oven to 350¡F. Spray 3-quart oval casserole with nonstick cooking spray.

CUT zucchini lengthwise in half. Cut crosswise into $\frac{1}{4}$-inch-thick slices. Combine spaghetti sauce, broth, zucchini, rice and mushrooms in prepared dish.

BAKE, covered, 30 minutes. Remove from oven and stir casserole. Cover and bake 15 to 20 minutes or until rice is tender. Remove from oven; sprinkle evenly with cheese. Bake, uncovered, 5 minutes or until cheese is melted. Garnish with yellow pepper, if desired.

Makes 6 servings

Cook's Nook

Arborio is an Italian-grown short-grain rice that has large, plump grains. It is used in risotto dishes because its high starch content produces a creamy texture and it can absorb more liquid than long-grain rice.

Italian Three-Cheese Macaroni

··

2 cups uncooked elbow
macaroni

4 tablespoons margarine or
butter

3 tablespoons all-purpose
flour

1 teaspoon dried Italian
seasoning

½ to 1 teaspoon black
pepper

½ teaspoon salt

2 cups milk

¾ cup (3 ounces) shredded
Cheddar cheese

¼ cup grated Parmesan
cheese

1 can (14½ ounces) diced
tomatoes, drained

1 cup (4 ounces) shredded
mozzarella cheese

½ cup dry bread crumbs
Fresh chives and oregano
sprig (optional)

PREHEAT oven to 350¡F. Spray 2-quart round casserole with nonstick cooking spray.

COOK pasta according to package directions until al dente. Drain and set aside.

Meanwhile, **MELT** margarine in medium saucepan over medium heat. Add flour, Italian seasoning, pepper and salt, stirring until smooth. Gradually add milk, stirring constantly until slightly thickened. Add Cheddar and Parmesan cheeses; stir until cheeses melt.

LAYER half of pasta, tomatoes and cheese sauce in prepared dish. Repeat layers.

COMBINE mozzarella cheese and bread crumbs in small bowl. Sprinkle evenly over casserole. Spray bread crumb mixture several times with cooking spray.

BAKE, covered, 30 minutes or until hot and bubbly. Uncover and bake 5 minutes or until top is golden brown. Garnish with chives and oregano, if desired. *Makes 4 servings*

Spinach-Cheese Pasta Casserole

8 ounces uncooked pasta shells

2 eggs

1 cup ricotta cheese

1 jar (26 ounces) marinara sauce

1 teaspoon salt

1 package (10 ounces) frozen chopped spinach, thawed and squeezed dry

1 cup (4 ounces) shredded mozzarella cheese

¼ cup grated Parmesan cheese

PREHEAT oven to 350¡F. Spray 1¹₂-quart round casserole with nonstick cooking spray.

COOK pasta according to package directions until al dente. Drain and set aside.

Meanwhile, **WHISK** eggs in large bowl until blended. Add ricotta cheese; stir until combined. Stir pasta, marinara sauce and salt in large bowl until pasta is well coated. Pour pasta mixture into prepared dish. Top with ricotta mixture and spinach. Sprinkle mozzarella and Parmesan cheeses evenly over casserole.

BAKE, covered, 30 minutes. Uncover and bake 15 minutes or until hot and bubbly.   *Makes 6 to 8 servings*

Potatoes au Gratin

．．

1½ pounds small red
    potatoes
  6 tablespoons margarine or
    butter, divided
  3 tablespoons all-purpose
    flour
  ½ teaspoon salt
  ¼ teaspoon ground white
    pepper

1½ cups milk
  1 cup (4 ounces) shredded
    Cheddar cheese
  4 green onions, thinly
    sliced
  ¾ cup cracker crumbs

PREHEAT oven to 350¡F. Spray 1-quart round casserole with nonstick cooking spray.

PLACE potatoes in 2-quart saucepan; add enough water to cover potatoes. Bring to a boil over high heat. Cook, uncovered, about 10 minutes or until partially done. *Potatoes should still be firm in center.* Drain and rinse in cold water until potatoes are cool. Drain and set aside.

Meanwhile, **MELT** 4 tablespoons margarine in medium saucepan over medium heat. Add flour, salt and pepper, stirring until smooth. Gradually add milk, stirring constantly until sauce is thickened. Add cheese, stirring until cheese is melted.

CUT potatoes crosswise into ^{1}₄-inch-thick slices. Layer one third of potatoes in prepared dish. Top with one third of onions and one third of cheese sauce. Repeat layers twice, ending with cheese sauce.

MELT remaining 2 tablespoons margarine. Combine cracker crumbs and margarine in small bowl. Sprinkle evenly over casserole.

BAKE, uncovered, 35 to 40 minutes or until hot and bubbly and potatoes are tender.   *Makes 4 to 6 servings*

Menu

Roast Beef

Potatoes au Gratin

Steamed Broccoli

Assorted Rolls

Apple Crisp with
Vanilla Ice Cream

Green Beans with Blue Cheese and Roasted Red Peppers

∙∙

1 bag (20 ounces) frozen cut green beans

½ jar roasted red pepper strips (about 3 ounces), drained and slivered

⅛ teaspoon salt

⅛ teaspoon ground white pepper

4 ounces cream cheese

½ cup milk

¾ cup (3 ounces) blue cheese, crumbled

½ cup Italian-style bread crumbs

1 tablespoon margarine or butter, melted

Red and yellow bell pepper rose and fresh Italian parsley (optional)

PREHEAT oven to 350¡F. Spray 2-quart oval casserole with nonstick cooking spray.

COMBINE green beans, red pepper strips, salt and white pepper in prepared dish.

PLACE cream cheese and milk in small saucepan; heat over low heat, stirring until melted. Add blue cheese; stir only until combined. Pour cheese mixture over green bean mixture and stir until green beans are coated.

COMBINE bread crumbs and margarine in small bowl; sprinkle evenly over casserole.

BAKE, uncovered, 20 minutes or until hot and bubbly. Garnish with bell peppers and Italian parsley, if desired. *Makes 4 servings*

Slow Cooker
Creations

Slow Cooker Creations

p. 94

p. 108

p. 142

p. 152

Savory Soups & Stews

Italian Beef and Barley Soup

1 boneless beef top sirloin steak (about 1½ pounds)
1 tablespoon vegetable oil
4 medium carrots or parsnips, sliced ¼-inch thick
1 cup chopped onion
1 teaspoon dried thyme leaves
½ teaspoon dried rosemary
¼ teaspoon black pepper
⅓ cup pearl barley
2 cans (14½ ounces each) beef broth
1 can (14½ ounces) diced tomatoes with Italian seasoning, undrained

Slow Cooker Directions

1. Cut beef into 1-inch pieces. Heat oil over medium-high heat in large skillet and brown beef on all sides. Set aside.

2. Place carrots and onion in slow cooker; sprinkle with thyme, rosemary and pepper. Top with barley and meat. Pour broth and tomatoes with juice over meat.

3. Cover; cook on LOW 8 to 10 hours.   *Makes 6 servings*

Prep Time: 20 minutes
Cook Time: 8 to 10 hours (LOW)

Italian Beef and Barley Soup

Easy Slow-Cooked Chili

2 pounds lean ground beef
2 tablespoons chili powder
1 tablespoon ground cumin
1 can (28 ounces) crushed tomatoes in purée, undrained
1 can (15 ounces) red kidney beans, drained and rinsed
1 cup water
2 cups *French's*® French Fried Onions, divided
¼ cup *Frank's*® *RedHot*® Original Cayenne Pepper Sauce
   Sour cream and shredded Cheddar cheese

Slow Cooker Directions

1. Cook ground beef, chili powder and cumin in large nonstick skillet over medium heat until browned, stirring frequently; drain. Transfer to slow cooker.

2. Stir in tomatoes with juice, beans, water, *½ cup* French Fried Onions and *Frank's RedHot* Sauce.

3. Cover; cook on LOW setting for 6 hours (or on HIGH for 3 hours). Serve chili topped with sour cream, cheese and remaining onions.

Makes 8 servings

Variation: For added Cheddar flavor, substitute *French's*® **Cheddar French Fried Onions** for the original flavor.

Prep Time: 10 minutes
Cook Time: 6 hours

Easy Slow-Cooked Chili

Chicken and Wild Rice Soup

3 cans (14½ ounces each) chicken broth
1 pound boneless skinless chicken breasts or thighs, cut into
    bite-size pieces
2 cups water
1 cup sliced celery
1 cup diced carrots
1 package (6 ounces) converted long grain and wild rice mix with
    seasoning packet (not quick-cooking or instant rice)
½ cup chopped onion
½ teaspoon black pepper
2 teaspoons white vinegar (optional)
1 tablespoon dried parsley flakes

Slow Cooker Directions

1. Combine broth, water, chicken, celery, carrots, rice and seasoning packet, onion and pepper in slow cooker; mix well.

2. Cover; cook on LOW 6 to 7 hours or on HIGH 4 to 5 hours or until chicken is tender.

3. Stir in vinegar, if desired. Garnish with parsley; serve.

Makes 9 (1½-cup) servings

Prep Time: 20 minutes
Cook Time: 6 to 7 hours

Chicken and Wild Rice Soup

Mushroom-Beef Stew

1 pound beef for stew
1 can (10¾ ounces) condensed cream of mushroom soup, undiluted
2 cans (4 ounces each) sliced mushrooms, drained
1 package (1 ounce) dry onion soup mix

Slow Cooker Directions
Combine all ingredients in slow cooker. Cover; cook on LOW 8 to 10 hours. Garnish as desired.   *Makes 4 servings*

Serving Suggestion: Serve this stew over hot cooked seasoned noodles or rice.

Easy Corn Chowder

2 cans (14½ ounces each) chicken broth
1 bag (16 ounces) frozen corn kernels
3 small potatoes, peeled and cut into ½-inch cubes
1 red bell pepper, diced
1 medium onion, diced
1 rib celery, sliced
½ teaspoon salt
½ teaspoon black pepper
¼ teaspoon ground coriander
½ cup heavy cream
8 slices bacon, crisp-cooked and crumbled

Slow Cooker Directions
1. Place broth, corn, potatoes, bell pepper, onion, celery, salt, black pepper and coriander into slow cooker. Cover; cook on LOW 7 to 8 hours.

2. Partially mash soup mixture with potato masher to thicken. Stir in cream; cook on HIGH, uncovered, about 30 minutes or until hot. Adjust seasonings, if desired. Garnish with bacon.   *Makes 6 servings*

Prep Time: 15 minutes
Cook Time: 7 to 8 hours

Mushroom-Beef Stew

Pasta Fagioli Soup

2 cans (14½ ounces each) reduced-sodium beef broth
1 can (16 ounces) Great Northern beans, rinsed and drained
1 can (14½ ounces) diced tomatoes, undrained
2 medium zucchini, quartered lengthwise and sliced
1 tablespoon olive oil
1½ teaspoons minced garlic
½ teaspoon dried basil leaves
½ teaspoon dried oregano leaves
½ cup tubetti, ditilini or small shell pasta, uncooked
½ cup garlic seasoned croutons
½ cup grated Asiago or Romano cheese
3 tablespoons chopped fresh basil or Italian parsley (optional)

Slow Cooker Directions

1. Combine broth, beans, tomatoes with juice, zucchini, oil, garlic, dried basil and oregano in slow cooker; mix well. Cover; cook on LOW 3 to 4 hours.

2. Stir in pasta. Cover; continue cooking on LOW 1 hour or until pasta is tender.

3. Serve soup with croutons and cheese. Garnish with fresh basil, if desired.

Makes 5 to 6 servings

Prep Time: 12 minutes
Cook Time: 4 to 5 hours

Pasta Fagioli Soup

Great Chili

1½ pounds ground beef
1½ cups chopped onion
1 cup chopped green bell pepper
2 cloves garlic, minced
3 cans (15 ounces each) dark red kidney beans, rinsed and drained
2 cans (15 ounces each) tomato sauce
1 can (14½ ounces) diced tomatoes, undrained
2 to 3 teaspoons chili powder
1 to 2 teaspoons dry hot mustard powder
¾ teaspoon dried basil leaves
½ teaspoon black pepper
1 to 2 dried hot chili peppers (optional)

Slow Cooker Directions

1. Cook and stir ground beef, onion, bell pepper and garlic in large skillet until meat is browned and onion is tender. Drain excess fat. Place beef mixture in slow cooker.

2. Add kidney beans, tomato sauce, tomatoes with juice, chili powder, mustard, basil, black pepper and chili peppers, if desired; mix well. If using chili pepper, remove and discard before serving chili.

3. Cover; cook on LOW 8 to 10 hours or on HIGH 4 to 5 hours.

Makes 6 servings

Tip

Serve this tasty chili with cornbread sticks or muffins.

Great Chili

Winter's Best Bean Soup

    6 ounces bacon, diced
   10 cups chicken broth
    3 cans (15 ounces each) Great Northern beans, drained
    1 can (14½ ounces) diced tomatoes, undrained
    1 large onion, chopped
    1 package (10 ounces) frozen sliced or diced carrots
    2 teaspoons bottled minced garlic
    1 fresh rosemary sprig *or* 1 teaspoon dried rosemary
    1 teaspoon black pepper

Slow Cooker Directions

1. Cook bacon in medium skillet over medium-high heat until just cooked; drain and transfer to slow cooker. Add remaining ingredients.

2. Cover; cook on LOW 8 hours or until beans are tender. Remove rosemary sprig and mince the leaves before serving.   *Makes 8 to 10 servings*

Serving Suggestion: Place slices of toasted Italian bread in bottom of individual soup bowls. Drizzle with olive oil. Pour soup over bread and serve.

Prep Time: 15 minutes
Cook Time: 8 hours (LOW)

Winter's Best Bean Soup

Slow Cooked Chicken & Wild Rice Soup

½ cup uncooked wild rice, rinsed thoroughly
2 medium carrots, peeled and shredded
2 stalks celery, thinly sliced
1 large yellow onion, chopped
5½ cups water
2 tablespoons HERB-OX® chicken flavored bouillon granules
1 cup heavy whipping cream
2 tablespoons all-purpose flour
2 (10-ounce) cans HORMEL® chunk breast of chicken
Slivered almonds, for garnish

In large (6-quart) slow cooker, combine all ingredients except heavy cream, flour and chunk chicken. Cover and cook on LOW heat setting for 4 hours or until rice is tender. Just before serving, combine heavy cream and flour. Slowly stir cream mixture into soup and add chunk chicken. Cook and stir constantly for 5 minutes or until mixture is slightly thickened and chicken is heated through. Ladle into bowls and garnish with slivered almonds.

Makes 6 to 8 servings

❧ Tip ❧

Wild rice should be thoroughly rinsed before cooking to remove any debris remaining after processing. To rinse, place raw rice in a bowl with cold water, stir and allow it to sit until the debris floats to the surface. Remove the debris and drain. Wild rice requires longer cooking than other rices. Avoid overcooking, because it will lose its characteristic chewy texture.

Tortilla Soup

   2 cans (14½ ounces each) chicken broth
   1 can (14½ ounces) diced tomatoes with jalapeño peppers,
       undrained
   2 cups chopped carrots
   2 cups frozen whole kernel corn
1½ cups chopped onion
   1 can (8 ounces) tomato sauce
   1 tablespoon chili powder
   1 teaspoon ground cumin
   ¼ teaspoon garlic powder
   2 cups chopped cooked chicken (optional)
       Shredded Monterey Jack cheese
       Tortilla chips, broken

Slow Cooker Directions

1. Combine broth, tomatoes with juice, carrots, corn, onion, tomato sauce, chili powder, cumin and garlic powder in slow cooker. Cover; cook on LOW 6 to 8 hours.

2. Stir in chicken, if desired. Ladle into bowls. Top each serving with cheese and tortilla chips.   *Makes 6 servings*

Prep Time: 10 minutes
Cook Time: 6 to 8 hours

Navy Bean & Ham Soup

   6 cups water
   5 cups dried navy beans, soaked overnight and drained
   1 pound ham, cubed
   1 can (15 ounces) corn, drained
   1 can (4 ounces) mild diced green chilies, drained
   1 onion, diced
       Salt and black pepper to taste

Slow Cooker Directions

Place all ingredients in slow cooker. Cover; cook on LOW 8 to 10 hours or until beans are softened.   *Makes 6 servings.*

Serving Suggestion: Serve this soup with biscuits.

Slow Cooker Cheese Soup

2 cans (10¾ ounces each) condensed cream of celery soup,
    undiluted
4 cups (1 pound) shredded Cheddar cheese
1 teaspoon paprika
1 teaspoon Worcestershire sauce
1¼ cups half-and-half
    Salt and black pepper

Slow Cooker Directions

1. Combine soup, cheese, paprika and Worcestershire sauce in slow cooker.

2. Cover; cook on LOW 2 to 3 hours.

3. Add half-and-half; stir to combine. Cover; cook another 20 minutes.
Season with salt and pepper to taste. Garnish as desired.

Makes 4 servings

Crockpot Beef Stew

2 pounds lean beef for stew, cut into 1-inch pieces
⅓ cup all-purpose flour
4 medium potatoes, peeled and cut into 1-inch pieces
3 to 4 celery stalks cut into ½-inch slices
3 to 4 carrots, peeled and cut into 1-inch slices
1 large onion, cut into wedges
1 can (8 ounces) tomato sauce
1 can (16 ounces) whole tomatoes, chopped
1½ tablespoons MRS. DASH® All-Purpose Original Blend
1 bay leaf

Slow Cooker Directions

Coat beef pieces with flour. Combine beef, vegetables and All-Purpose
Original Blend in slow cooker; mix well. Add tomato sauce and chopped
tomatoes; stir gently to mix. Add bay leaf. Cover and cook at HIGH for
5 to 6 hours or at LOW for 11 to 12 hours. Remove bay leaf. Stir and serve.

Makes 8 servings

Prep Time: 20 minutes
Cook Time: 6 hours

Slow Cooker Cheese Soup

Slow-Cooker Chili Mac

1 pound ground beef or turkey
1 can (14½ ounces) diced tomatoes, drained
1 cup chopped onion
1 clove garlic, minced
1 tablespoon chili powder
½ teaspoon salt
½ teaspoon ground cumin
½ teaspoon dried oregano leaves
¼ teaspoon red pepper flakes
¼ teaspoon black pepper
8 ounces Reduced Carb Elbows (4 cups cooked)
Grated Cheddar cheese (optional)

1. Brown ground beef in large skillet over medium heat until no longer pink, stirring to break up meat; drain off fat. Place cooked beef in slow cooker with remaining ingredients except elbows and cheese. Mix well. Cook on LOW 4 hours.

2. Cook elbows according to package directions; drain. Stir in cooked elbows and cook on LOW 1 hour more. Top each serving with grated cheese, if desired. *Makes 10 servings*

Favorite recipe from American Italian Pasta Company.

Slow-Cooker Chili Mac

Peppery Potato Soup

2 cans (14½ ounces each) chicken broth
4 small baking potatoes, halved and sliced
1 large onion, quartered and sliced
1 rib celery with leaves, sliced
¼ cup all-purpose flour
¾ teaspoon black pepper
½ teaspoon salt
1 cup half-and-half
1 tablespoon butter
   Celery leaves and fresh parsley (optional)

Slow Cooker Directions

1. Combine broth, potatoes, onion, celery, flour, pepper and salt in slow cooker; mix well. Cover; cook on LOW 6 to 7½ hours.

2. Stir in half-and-half; cover and continue to cook 1 hour.

3. Remove slow cooker lid. Slightly crush potato mixture with potato masher. Continue to cook, uncovered, an additional 30 minutes until slightly thickened. Just before serving, stir in butter. Garnish with celery leaves and parsley, if desired.   *Makes 6 (1¼-cup) servings*

Prep Time: 15 minutes
Cook Time: 6 to 8 hours

Peppery Potato Soup

Beef Fajita Soup

1 pound beef for stew
1 can (15 ounces) pinto beans, rinsed and drained
1 can (15 ounces) black beans, rinsed and drained
1 can (14½ ounces) diced tomatoes with roasted garlic, undrained
1 can (14 ounces) beef broth
1 small green bell pepper, thinly sliced
1 small red bell pepper, thinly sliced
1 small onion, thinly sliced
1½ cups water
2 teaspoons ground cumin
1 teaspoon seasoned salt
1 teaspoon black pepper
  Toppings: sour cream, shredded Monterey Jack or Cheddar
    cheese, chopped olives

Slow Cooker Directions

1. Combine beef, beans, tomatoes with juice, broth, bell peppers, onion, water, cumin, salt and black pepper in slow cooker.

2. Cover; cook on LOW 8 hours or until beef is tender.

3. Serve with suggested toppings.   *Makes 8 servings*

Serving Suggestion: This soup is excellent served with a crusty loaf of brown bread.

Beef Fajita Soup

Main Dish Meats

🌷 🌷 🌷 🌷

Fiery Chili Beef

1 beef flank steak (1 to 1½ pounds)
1 can (28 ounces) diced tomatoes, undrained
1 can (15 ounces) pinto beans, rinsed and drained
1 medium onion, chopped
2 cloves garlic, minced
½ teaspoon salt
½ teaspoon ground cumin
¼ teaspoon black pepper
1 canned chipotle chile pepper in adobo sauce
1 teaspoon adobo sauce from canned chile pepper
   Flour tortillas

Slow Cooker Directions

1. Cut flank steak in 6 serving-sized pieces. Place flank steak, tomatoes with juice, beans, onion, garlic, salt, cumin and black pepper into slow cooker.

2. Dice chile pepper. Add pepper and adobo sauce to slow cooker; mix well.

3. Cover; cook on LOW 7 to 8 hours. Serve with tortillas.

Makes 6 servings

Tip: Chipotle chile peppers are dried, smoked jalapeño peppers with a very hot yet smoky, sweet flavor. They can be found dried, pickled and canned in adobo sauce.

Prep Time: 15 minutes
Cook Time: 7 to 8 hours (LOW)

Fiery Chili Beef

Shredded Apricot Pork Sandwiches

2 medium onions, thinly sliced
1 cup apricot preserves
½ cup barbecue sauce
½ cup packed dark brown sugar
¼ cup cider vinegar
2 tablespoons Worcestershire sauce
½ teaspoon red pepper flakes
1 (4-pound) boneless pork loin roast, trimmed of fat
¼ cup cold water
2 tablespoons cornstarch
1 tablespoon grated fresh ginger
1 teaspoon salt
1 teaspoon black pepper
10 to 12 sesame or onion rolls, toasted

Slow Cooker Directions

1. Combine onions, preserves, barbecue sauce, brown sugar, vinegar, Worcestershire sauce and pepper flakes in small bowl. Place pork roast in slow cooker. Pour apricot mixture over roast. Cover; cook on LOW 8 to 9 hours.

2. Remove pork from cooking liquid to cutting board; cool slightly. Using 2 forks, shred pork into coarse shreds. Let cooking liquid stand 5 minutes to allow fat to rise. Skim fat.

3. Combine water, cornstarch, ginger, salt and pepper; blend well. Whisk cornstarch mixture into slow cooker liquid. Cook on HIGH 15 to 30 minutes or until thickened. Return pork to slow cooker. Serve over rolls.

Makes 10 to 12 sandwiches

Variation: 1 (4-pound) pork shoulder roast, cut into pieces and trimmed of fat, can be substituted for pork loin roast.

*Shredded Apricot Pork
Sandwich*

Beef Bourguignon

1 to 2 boneless beef top sirloin steaks (about 3 pounds)
½ cup all-purpose flour
4 slices bacon, diced
2 medium carrots, diced
8 small new red potatoes, unpeeled, cut into quarters
8 to 10 mushrooms, sliced
20 to 24 pearl onions
3 cloves garlic, minced
1 bay leaf
1 teaspoon dried marjoram leaves
½ teaspoon dried thyme leaves
½ teaspoon salt
   Black pepper
2½ cups Burgundy wine or beef broth

Slow Cooker Directions

1. Cut beef into ½-inch pieces. Coat with flour, shaking off excess; set aside. Cook bacon in large skillet over medium heat until partially cooked. Add beef; cook until browned. Remove beef and bacon with slotted spoon.

2. Layer carrots, potatoes, mushrooms, onions, garlic, bay leaf, marjoram, thyme, salt, pepper to taste and beef and bacon mixture in slow cooker. Pour wine over all.

3. Cover; cook on LOW 8 to 9 hours or until beef is tender. Remove and discard bay leaf before serving.   *Makes 10 to 12 servings*

Beef Bourguignon

Sweet 'n' Spicy Ribs

5 cups barbecue sauce*
¾ cup brown sugar
¼ cup honey
2 tablespoons Cajun seasoning
1 tablespoon garlic powder
1 tablespoon onion powder
6 pounds pork or beef back ribs, cut into 3-rib portions

Barbecue sauce adds a significant flavor to this recipe. Use your favorite sauce to ensure you fully enjoy the dish.

Slow Cooker Directions

1. Stir together barbecue sauce, brown sugar, honey, Cajun seasoning, garlic powder and onion powder in medium bowl. Remove 1 cup mixture; refrigerate and reserve for dipping sauce.

2. Place ribs in slow cooker. Pour barbecue sauce mixture over ribs. Cover; cook on LOW 8 hours or until meat is very tender.

3. Uncover; remove ribs. Skim fat from sauce. Serve with reserved sauce.

Makes 10 servings

Tip

This dish is excellent over rice.

Sweet 'n' Spicy Ribs

Spanish-Style Couscous

1 pound lean ground beef
1 can (about 14 ounces) beef broth
1 small green bell pepper, cut into ½-inch pieces
½ cup pimiento-stuffed green olives, sliced
½ medium onion, chopped
2 cloves garlic, minced
1 teaspoon ground cumin
½ teaspoon dried thyme leaves
1⅓ cups water
1 cup uncooked couscous

Slow Cooker Directions

1. Heat skillet over high heat until hot. Add beef; cook until browned. Pour off fat. Place broth, bell pepper, olives, onion, garlic, cumin, thyme and beef in slow cooker.

2. Cover; cook on LOW 4 hours or until bell pepper is tender.

3. Bring water to a boil over high heat in small saucepan. Stir in couscous. Cover; remove from heat. Let stand 5 minutes; fluff with fork. Spoon couscous onto plates; top with beef mixture.   *Makes 4 servings*

Spanish-Style Couscous

Cabbage Rolls

    1 large head cabbage, cored
      Salt
    3 pounds ground beef
    1 pound pork sausage
    2 medium onions, chopped
  1½ cups cooked rice
    1 egg
    2 tablespoons prepared horseradish
    2 tablespoons ketchup
    1 package (about 1 ounce) dry onion soup mix
    1 tablespoon salt
    1 teaspoon allspice
  ½ teaspoon garlic powder
      Black pepper
      Sauce for Cabbage Rolls (recipe follows)

Slow Cooker Directions

1. In large stockpot filled halfway with salted water, place cabbage core-side down. Simmer over medium heat 5 minutes or until outside leaves come off easily. Continue to simmer and pull out rest of leaves. Set aside; reserve cabbage water.

2. Stir together remaining ingredients in large mixing bowl. Roll meat mixture into 3-inch balls. Place one meat ball into each cabbage leaf; roll up, fold in edges and secure with toothpick. Continue with remaining cabbage rolls.

3. Place cabbage rolls in slow cooker. Cover; cook on LOW 6 to 8 hours. Prepare Sauce for Cabbage Rolls. Pour sauce over top of rolls.

Makes 16 servings

Sauce for Cabbage Rolls

    3 cans (10¾ ounces each) condensed cheese soup, undiluted
    1 can (10¾ ounces) condensed tomato soup, undiluted
  2½ cups reserved cabbage water

Heat all ingredients in medium saucepan over medium heat until warm.

Peachy Pork

2 cans (about 15 ounces each) sliced peaches in heavy syrup,
    undrained
6 to 8 boneless pork blade or top loin chops (about 2 pounds)
1 small onion, thinly sliced
½ cup golden raisins
¼ cup packed light brown sugar
3 tablespoons cider vinegar
2 tablespoons tapioca
1 teaspoon salt
¾ teaspoon ground cinnamon
¼ teaspoon red pepper flakes
2 tablespoons cornstarch
2 tablespoons water

Slow Cooker Directions

1. Cut peach slices in half with spoon. Place peaches with juice, pork chops, onion, raisins, sugar, vinegar, tapioca, salt, cinnamon and pepper flakes into slow cooker. Cover; cook on LOW 7 to 8 hours.

2. Remove pork to warm platter. Skim off fat from peach mixture. Combine cornstarch and water to make smooth paste. Stir into peach mixture. Cook on HIGH 15 minutes or until sauce is thickened. Adjust seasonings, if desired.

Makes 6 to 8 servings

Prep Time: 15 minutes
Cook Time: 7 to 8 hours

Glazed Pork Loin

    1 bag (1 pound) baby carrots
    4 boneless pork loin chops
    1 jar (8 ounces) apricot preserves

Slow Cooker Directions

1. Place carrots in bottom of slow cooker. Place pork on carrots and brush with preserves.

2. Cover; cook on LOW 8 hours or on HIGH 4 hours.   *Makes 4 servings*

Serving Suggestion: Serve with seasoned or cheese-flavored instant mashed potatoes.

Slow Cooker Brisket of Beef

    1 whole well-trimmed beef brisket (about 5 pounds)
    2 teaspoons bottled minced garlic
    ½ teaspoon black pepper
    2 large onions, cut into ¼-inch slices and separated into rings
    1 bottle (12 ounces) chili sauce
   12 ounces beef broth, dark ale or water
    2 tablespoons Worcestershire sauce
    1 tablespoon packed brown sugar

Slow Cooker Directions

1. Place brisket, fat side down, in slow cooker. Spread garlic evenly over brisket; sprinkle with pepper. Arrange onions over brisket. Combine chili sauce, broth, Worcestershire sauce and sugar; pour over brisket and onions. Cover; cook on LOW for 8 hours.

2. Turn brisket over; stir onions into sauce and spoon over brisket. Add vegetables if desired. Cover; cook until fork-tender. Transfer brisket to cutting board. Tent with foil; let stand 10 minutes.

3. Stir juices in slow cooker. Spoon off and discard fat from juices. (Juices may be thinned to desired consistency with water or thickened by simmering, uncovered, in saucepan.) Carve brisket across grain into thin slices. Spoon juices over brisket.   *Makes 10 to 12 servings*

Glazed Pork Loin

Slow-Simmered Jambalaya

2 can (14½ ounces each) stewed tomatoes, undrained
2 cups diced boiled ham
2 medium onions, coarsely chopped
1 medium green bell pepper, diced
2 ribs celery, sliced
1 cup uncooked long-grain converted rice
2 tablespoons vegetable oil
2 tablespoons ketchup
3 cloves garlic, minced
½ teaspoon dried thyme leaves
½ teaspoon black pepper
⅛ teaspoon ground cloves
1 pound fresh or frozen uncooked shrimp, peeled and deveined

Slow Cooker Directions

1. Combine tomatoes with juice, ham, onions, bell pepper, celery, rice, oil, ketchup, garlic, thyme, black pepper and cloves in slow cooker.

2. Cover; cook on LOW 8 to 10 hours.

3. One hour before serving, turn slow cooker to HIGH. Stir in shrimp. Cover; cook until shrimp are pink and tender.   *Makes 4 to 6 servings*

⋙ *Tip* ⋘

*Keep the lid on! The slow cooker can take as long as
30 minutes to regain heat lost when the cover is removed.
Only remove the cover when instructed to do so by the
recipe.*

Slow-Simmered Jambalaya

Pork Roast Landaise

2 tablespoons olive oil
2½ pounds boneless center cut pork loin roast
   Salt and pepper
1 medium sweet onion, diced
2 large cloves garlic, minced
2 teaspoons dried thyme
2 cups chicken stock, divided
2 tablespoons cornstarch or arrowroot
¼ cup red wine vinegar
¼ cup sugar
½ cup port or sherry wine
2 parsnips, cut in ¾-inch slices
1½ cups pitted prunes
3 pears, cored and sliced ¾-inch thick

1. Heat olive oil in large saucepan over medium-high heat. Season pork roast with salt and pepper and brown in saucepan on all sides. Remove browned roast from pan and place in slow cooker.

2. Add onion and garlic to saucepan. Cook and stir over medium heat for 2 to 3 minutes. Stir in thyme. Add onion mixture to slow cooker.

3. Combine ¼ cup of chicken stock with the cornstarch in small bowl; set aside.

4. Combine vinegar and sugar in same saucepan in which onion and garlic were cooked. Cook over medium heat, stirring constantly, until mixture thickens into syrup. Add port and cook 1 minute more. Add remaining 1¾ cups chicken stock. Whisk in cornstarch mixture and cook until smooth and slightly thickened. Pour into slow cooker.

5. Cover; cook on LOW 8 hours or on HIGH 4 hours. During the last 30 minutes of cooking, add parsnips, prunes and pears. Serve over rice or mashed potatoes, if desired.   *Makes 4 to 6 servings*

Pork Roast Landaise

Pot Roast

1 tablespoon vegetable oil
1 beef chuck shoulder roast (3 to 4 pounds)
6 medium potatoes, halved
6 carrots, sliced
2 medium onions, quartered
2 ribs celery, sliced
1 can (14½ ounces) diced tomatoes, undrained
   Salt
   Black pepper
   Dried oregano leaves
   Water
1½ to 2 tablespoons all-purpose flour

Slow Cooker Directions

1. Heat oil in large skillet over medium-low heat. Add roast; brown on all sides. Drain excess fat.

2. Place roast in slow cooker. Add potatoes, carrots, onions, celery and tomatoes with juice. Season with salt, pepper and oregano to taste. Add enough water to cover bottom of slow cooker by about ½ inch. Cover; cook on LOW 8 to 10 hours.

3. Serve with cooked juices from slow cooker or to make gravy, combine juices with flour in small saucepan. Cook and stir over medium heat until thickened.

Makes 6 to 8 servings

Autumn Harvest Sausage and Cabbage

1 package (12 ounces) reduced-fat pork sausage
8 cups chopped red cabbage (1 small head)
3 potatoes, diced
3 apples, diced
1 onion, sliced
½ cup sugar
½ cup white vinegar
1 teaspoon salt
½ teaspoon black pepper
½ teaspoon ground allspice
¼ teaspoon ground cloves

Slow Cooker Directions

1. Cook sausage in large nonstick skillet over medium-high heat until no longer pink, stirring to separate; drain fat.

2. Combine sausage and remaining ingredients in large bowl; mix well. Spoon mixture into slow cooker. Cover; cook on LOW 8 to 10 hours or until potatoes are tender. *Makes 6 to 8 servings*

Note: It is easier to mix all the ingredients in a large bowl instead of the slow cooker because the slow cooker will be filled to the top until the cabbage cooks down.

Prep Time: 30 minutes
Cook Time: 8 to 10 hours

Sweet and Sour Spare Ribs

4 pounds pork spare ribs
2 cups dry sherry or chicken broth
½ cup pineapple, mango or guava juice
⅓ cup chicken broth
2 tablespoons packed light brown sugar
2 tablespoons cider vinegar
2 tablespoons soy sauce
1 clove garlic, minced
½ teaspoon salt
¼ teaspoon black pepper
⅛ teaspoon red pepper flakes
2 tablespoons cornstarch

Slow Cooker Directions

1. Preheat oven to 400°F. Place ribs in foil-lined shallow roasting pan. Bake 30 minutes, turning over after 15 minutes. Remove from oven. Slice meat into 2-rib portions. Place ribs in 5-quart slow cooker. Add remaining ingredients, except cornstarch, to slow cooker.

2. Cover; cook on LOW 6 hours. Transfer ribs to platter; keep warm. Let liquid in slow cooker stand 5 minutes to allow fat to rise. Skim off fat.

3. Combine cornstarch and ¼ cup liquid from slow cooker; stir until smooth. Stir mixture into liquid in slow cooker; mix well. Cook on HIGH 10 minutes or until slightly thickened. *Makes 4 servings*

Sweet and Sour Spare Ribs

Fiesta Rice and Sausage

1 teaspoon vegetable oil

2 pounds spicy Italian sausage, casing removed

2 cloves garlic, minced

2 teaspoons ground cumin

4 onions, chopped

4 green bell peppers, chopped

3 jalapeño peppers,* seeded and minced

4 cups beef broth

2 packages (6¼ ounces each) long-grain and wild rice mix

Jalapeño peppers can sting and irritate the skin; wear rubber gloves when handling peppers and do not touch eyes. Wash hands after handling.

Slow Cooker Directions

1. Heat oil in large skillet over medium-high heat; brown sausage about 5 minutes, stirring to separate. Add garlic and cumin; cook 30 seconds. Add onions, bell peppers and jalapeño peppers. Cook and stir until onions are tender, about 10 minutes. Pour mixture into slow cooker.

2. Stir in beef broth and rice.

3. Cover; cook on LOW 4 to 6 hours or on HIGH 1 to 2 hours.

Makes 10 to 12 servings

Tip

To make cleanup easier, spray the inside of the slow cooker with nonstick cooking spray before adding the food.

Fiesta Rice and Sausage

Perfect Poultry

Easy Chicken Alfredo

1½ pounds chicken breast, cut into ½-inch pieces
1 medium onion, chopped
1 tablespoon dried chives
1 tablespoon dried basil leaves
1 tablespoon extra-virgin olive oil
1 teaspoon lemon pepper
¼ teaspoon ground ginger
½ pound broccoli, coarsely chopped
1 red bell pepper, chopped
1 can (8 ounces) sliced water chestnuts, drained
1 cup baby carrots
3 cloves garlic, minced
1 jar (16 ounces) Alfredo sauce
1 package (8 ounces) wide egg noodles, cooked and drained

Slow Cooker Directions

1. Combine chicken, onion, chives, basil, olive oil, lemon pepper and ginger in slow cooker; stir thoroughly. Add broccoli, bell pepper, water chestnuts, carrots and garlic. Mix well.

2. Cover; cook on LOW 8 hours or on HIGH 4 hours.

3. Add Alfredo sauce; cook on HIGH an additional 30 minutes or until heated through. Serve over hot cooked egg noodles.   *Makes 6 servings*

Easy Chicken Alfredo

Italian Chicken with Sausage and Peppers

2½ pounds chicken pieces
2 tablespoons olive oil
½ to ¾ pounds sweet Italian sausage
2 green bell peppers, chopped
1 onion, chopped
1 carrot, finely chopped
2 cloves garlic, minced
1 can (15 ounces) tomato sauce
1 can (19 ounces) condensed tomato soup, undiluted
¼ teaspoon dried oregano
¼ teaspoon dried basil
1 bay leaf
Salt and pepper

Slow Cooker Directions

1. Rinse chicken; pat dry. Heat oil in large skillet over medium-high heat. Add chicken, skin side down. Cook about 10 minutes, turning to brown both sides. Remove and set aside.

2. Add sausage to skillet and cook 4 to 5 minutes or until browned. Remove, cut into 1-inch pieces and set aside. Drain off all but 1 tablespoon fat from skillet.

3. Add bell peppers, onion, carrot and garlic to skillet. Cook 4 to 5 minutes or until vegetables are tender.

4. Add tomato sauce, tomato soup, oregano, basil and bay leaf; stir well. Season with salt and pepper. Transfer to slow cooker.

5. Add chicken and sausage to slow cooker. Cover; cook on LOW 6 to 8 hours or on HIGH 4 to 6 hours. Remove and discard bay leaf before serving.   *Makes 6 servings*

*Italian Chicken with
Sausage and Peppers*

Turkey Breast with Barley-Cranberry Stuffing

2 cups fat-free reduced-sodium chicken broth
1 cup uncooked quick-cooking barley
½ cup chopped onion
½ cup dried cranberries
2 tablespoons slivered almonds, toasted
½ teaspoon rubbed sage
½ teaspoon garlic-pepper seasoning
  Nonstick cooking spray
1 fresh or frozen bone-in turkey breast half (about 2 pounds),
  thawed and skinned
⅓ cup finely chopped fresh parsley

Slow Cooker Directions

1. Combine broth, barley, onion, cranberries, almonds, sage and garlic-pepper seasoning in slow cooker.

2. Spray large nonstick skillet with cooking spray. Heat over medium heat until hot. Brown turkey breast on all sides; add to slow cooker. Cover; cook on LOW 3 to 4 hours or until internal temperature of turkey reaches 170°F when tested with meat thermometer inserted into thickest part of breast, not touching bone.

3. Transfer turkey to cutting board; cover with foil and let stand 10 to 15 minutes before carving. Internal temperature will rise 5°F to 10°F during stand time. Stir parsley into sauce mixture in slow cooker. Serve sliced turkey with sauce and stuffing.   *Makes 6 servings*

Turkey Breast with Barley-Cranberry Stuffing

Coq au Vin

4 slices thick-cut bacon
2 cups frozen pearl onions, thawed
1 cup sliced button mushrooms
1 clove garlic, minced
1 teaspoon dried thyme leaves
⅛ teaspoon black pepper
6 boneless skinless chicken breast halves (about 2 pounds)
½ cup dry red wine
¾ cup reduced-sodium chicken broth
¼ cup tomato paste
3 tablespoons all-purpose flour
　　Hot cooked egg noodles (optional)

Slow Cooker Directions

1. Cook bacon in medium skillet over medium heat. Drain and crumble. Layer ingredients in slow cooker in the following order: onions, bacon, mushrooms, garlic, thyme, pepper, chicken, wine and broth.

2. Cover; cook on LOW 6 to 8 hours.

3. Remove chicken and vegetables; cover and keep warm. Ladle ½ cup cooking liquid into small bowl; allow to cool slightly. Turn slow cooker to HIGH; cover. Mix reserved liquid, tomato paste and flour until smooth. Return mixture to slow cooker; cover and cook 15 minutes or until thickened. Serve over hot noodles, if desired.　　　　*Makes 6 servings*

Coq au Vin

Fusilli Pizzaiola with Turkey Meatballs

2 cans (14½ ounces each) no-salt-added tomatoes, undrained
1 can (8 ounces) no-salt-added tomato sauce
¼ cup chopped onion
¼ cup grated carrot
2 tablespoons no-salt-added tomato paste
2 tablespoons chopped fresh basil
1 clove garlic, minced
½ teaspoon dried thyme leaves
¼ teaspoon sugar
¼ teaspoon black pepper, divided
1 bay leaf
1 pound ground turkey breast
1 egg, lightly beaten
1 tablespoon fat-free (skim) milk
¼ cup Italian-seasoned dry bread crumbs
2 tablespoons chopped fresh parsley
8 ounces uncooked fusilli or other spiral-shaped pasta

Slow Cooker Directions

1. Combine tomatoes with juice, tomato sauce, onion, carrot, tomato paste, basil, garlic, thyme, sugar, ⅛ teaspoon black pepper and bay leaf in slow cooker. Break up tomatoes gently with wooden spoon. Cover; cook on LOW 4½ to 5 hours.

2. About 45 minutes before end of cooking, prepare meatballs. Preheat oven to 350°F. Combine turkey, egg and milk; blend in bread crumbs, parsley and remaining ⅛ teaspoon black pepper. With wet hands, shape mixture into small balls. Spray baking sheet with nonstick cooking spray. Arrange meatballs on baking sheet. Bake 25 minutes or until no longer pink in center.

3. Add meatballs to slow cooker. Cover and cook 45 minutes to 1 hour or until meatballs are heated through. Remove and discard bay leaf. Prepare pasta according to package directions; drain. Place in serving bowl; top with meatballs and sauce.   *Makes 4 servings*

Tuscan Pasta

1 pound boneless skinless chicken breasts, cut into 1-inch pieces
1 can (15½ ounces) red kidney beans, rinsed and drained
1 can (15 ounces) tomato sauce
2 cans (14½ ounces each) Italian-style stewed tomatoes
1 medium green bell pepper, chopped
1 jar (4½ ounces) sliced mushrooms, drained
½ cup chopped onion
½ cup chopped celery
4 cloves garlic, minced
1 cup water
1 teaspoon Italian seasoning
6 ounces uncooked thin spaghetti, broken in half

Slow Cooker Directions

1. Place all ingredients except spaghetti in slow cooker.

2. Cover; cook on LOW 4 hours or until vegetables are tender.

3. Turn slow cooker to HIGH. Stir in spaghetti; cover. Stir again after 10 minutes. Cover; cook 45 minutes or until pasta is tender. Garnish with basil and bell pepper strips, if desired. *Makes 8 servings*

Tuscan Pasta

Slow-Simmered Curried Chicken

1½ cups chopped onions
1 medium green bell pepper, chopped
1 pound boneless skinless chicken breast or thighs, cut into
    bite-size pieces
1 cup medium salsa
2 teaspoons grated fresh ginger
½ teaspoon garlic powder
½ teaspoon red pepper flakes
¼ cup chopped fresh cilantro
1 teaspoon sugar
1 teaspoon curry powder
¾ teaspoon salt
    Hot cooked rice

Slow Cooker Directions

1. Place onions and bell pepper in bottom of slow cooker. Top with chicken. Combine salsa, ginger, garlic powder and pepper flakes in small bowl; spoon over chicken.

2. Cover; cook on LOW 5 to 6 hours or until chicken is tender.

3. Combine cilantro, sugar, curry powder and salt in small bowl. Stir mixture into slow cooker. Cover; cook on HIGH 15 minutes or until hot. Serve with rice. *Makes 4 servings*

Prep Time: 15 to 20 minutes
Cook Time: 5 to 6 hours (LOW)

*Slow-Simmered Curried
Chicken*

Greek-Style Chicken

6 boneless skinless chicken thighs
½ teaspoon salt
½ teaspoon black pepper
1 tablespoon olive oil
½ cup chicken broth
1 lemon, thinly sliced
¼ cup pitted kalamata olives
½ teaspoon dried oregano leaves
1 clove garlic, minced
    Hot cooked orzo or rice

Slow Cooker Directions

1. Remove visible fat from chicken; sprinkle chicken thighs with salt and pepper. Heat oil in large skillet over medium-high heat. Brown chicken on all sides. Place in slow cooker.

2. Add broth, lemon, olives, oregano and garlic to slow cooker.

3. Cover; cook on LOW 5 to 6 hours or until chicken is tender. Serve with orzo.   *Makes 4 to 6 servings*

Prep Time: 15 minutes
Cook Time: 5 to 6 hours

Greek-Style Chicken

Southwestern-Style Chicken

6 to 8 boneless skinless chicken thighs or breasts
1 package (about 1¼ ounces) taco seasoning mix
¼ cup flour
2 tablespoons vegetable oil
1 large onion, cut into 1-inch pieces
2 green peppers, cut into 1-inch pieces
1 can (14½ ounces) diced tomatoes with jalapeños, undrained
   Salt and pepper

Slow Cooker Directions

1. Trim visible fat from chicken.

2. Reserve 1 teaspoon taco seasoning. Combine flour and remaining seasoning in plastic food storage bag. Add chicken, 1 to 2 pieces at a time; shake to coat.

3. Heat oil in large skillet over medium-high heat; brown chicken. Transfer chicken to slow cooker; sprinkle with reserved seasoning.

4. Add onion to skillet; cook and stir until translucent. Transfer onion to slow cooker. Add green peppers and tomatoes with juice. Cover; cook on LOW 6 to 7 hours or until chicken is tender. Season with salt and pepper to taste.   *Makes 4 to 6 servings*

Prep Time: 20 minutes
Cook Time: 6 to 7 hours

Turkey Tacos

1 pound ground turkey
1 medium onion, chopped
1 can (6 ounces) tomato paste
½ cup chunky salsa
1 tablespoon chopped fresh cilantro
½ teaspoon salt
1 tablespoon butter
1 tablespoon all-purpose flour
¼ teaspoon salt
⅓ cup milk
½ cup sour cream
   Ground red pepper
8 taco shells

Slow Cooker Directions

1. Brown turkey and onion in large skillet over medium heat, stirring to separate meat. Combine turkey mixture, tomato paste, salsa, cilantro and salt in slow cooker. Cover; cook on LOW 4 to 5 hours.

2. Just before serving, melt butter in small saucepan over low heat. Stir in flour and salt; cook 1 minute. Carefully stir in milk. Cook and stir over low heat until thickened. Remove from heat. Combine sour cream and dash of ground red pepper in small bowl. Stir into hot milk mixture. Return to heat; cook over low heat 1 minute, stirring constantly.

3. Spoon ¼ cup turkey mixture into each taco shell; keep warm. Spoon sour cream mixture over taco filling.

Makes 8 tacos

Chicken Stew with Dumplings

2 cans (about 14 ounces each) chicken broth, divided
2 cups sliced carrots
1 cup chopped onion
1 large green bell pepper, sliced
½ cup sliced celery
⅔ cup all-purpose flour
1 pound boneless skinless chicken breasts, cut into 1-inch pieces
1 large potato, unpeeled and cut into 1-inch pieces
6 ounces mushrooms, halved
¾ cup frozen peas
1 teaspoon dried basil leaves
¾ teaspoon dried rosemary leaves
¼ teaspoon dried tarragon leaves
¾ to 1 teaspoon salt
¼ teaspoon black pepper
¼ cup heavy cream

Herb Dumplings
1 cup biscuit baking mix
¼ teaspoon *each* dried basil and rosemary leaves
⅛ teaspoon dried tarragon leaves
⅓ cup reduced-fat (2%) milk

Slow Cooker Directions

1. Reserve 1 cup chicken broth. Combine carrots, onion, green bell pepper, celery and remaining chicken broth in slow cooker. Cover; cook on LOW 2 hours.

2. Stir flour into remaining 1 cup broth until smooth. Stir into slow cooker. Add chicken, potato, mushrooms, peas, 1 teaspoon basil, ¾ teaspoon rosemary and ¼ teaspoon tarragon to slow cooker. Cover; cook 4 hours or until vegetables are tender and chicken is no longer pink in center. Stir in salt, black pepper and heavy cream.

3. Combine baking mix, ¼ teaspoon basil, ¼ teaspoon rosemary and ¼ teaspoon tarragon in small bowl. Stir in milk to form soft dough. Spoon dumpling mixture on top of stew in 4 large spoonfuls. Cook, uncovered, 30 minutes. Cover; cook 30 to 45 minutes or until dumplings are firm and toothpick inserted in center comes out clean.   *Makes 4 servings*

Chicken Stew with Dumplings

Thai Turkey & Noodles

1 package (about 1½ pounds) turkey tenderloins, cut into ¾-inch
  pieces
1 red bell pepper, cut into short, thin strips
1¼ cups reduced-sodium chicken broth, divided
¼ cup reduced-sodium soy sauce
3 cloves garlic, minced
¾ teaspoon red pepper flakes
¼ teaspoon salt
2 tablespoons cornstarch
3 green onions, cut into ½-inch pieces
⅓ cup creamy or chunky peanut butter (not natural-style)
12 ounces hot cooked vermicelli pasta
¾ cup peanuts or cashews, chopped
¾ cup cilantro, chopped

Slow Cooker Directions

1. Place turkey, bell pepper, 1 cup broth, soy sauce, garlic, red pepper flakes
and salt in slow cooker. Cover; cook on LOW 3 hours.

2. Mix cornstarch with remaining ¼ cup broth in small bowl until smooth.
Turn slow cooker to HIGH. Stir in green onions, peanut butter and
cornstarch mixture. Cover; cook 30 minutes or until sauce is thickened and
turkey is no longer pink in center. Stir well.

3. Serve over vermicelli. Sprinkle with peanuts and cilantro.

Makes 6 servings

Tip

*If you don't have vermicelli on hand, try substituting
ramen noodles. Discard the flavor packet from ramen
soup mix and drop the noodles into boiling water. Cook
the noodles 2 to 3 minutes or until just tender. Drain and
serve hot.*

Thai Turkey & Noodles

Meatless Entrées

Vegetable Pasta Sauce

2 cans (14½ ounces each) diced tomatoes, undrained
1 can (14½ ounces) whole tomatoes, undrained
1½ cups sliced mushrooms
1 medium red bell pepper, diced
1 medium green bell pepper, diced
1 small yellow squash, cut into ¼-inch slices
1 small zucchini, cut into ¼-inch slices
1 can (6 ounces) tomato paste
4 green onions, sliced
2 tablespoons dried Italian seasoning
1 tablespoon chopped fresh parsley
3 cloves garlic, minced
1 teaspoon salt
1 teaspoon red pepper flakes (optional)
1 teaspoon black pepper
  Hot cooked pasta
  Parmesan cheese and fresh basil for garnish (optional)

Slow Cooker Directions
Combine all ingredients except pasta and garnishes in slow cooker, stirring until well blended. Cover; cook on LOW 6 to 8 hours. Serve over cooked pasta. Garnish with Parmesan cheese and fresh basil, if desired.

Makes 4 to 6 servings

Vegetable Pasta Sauce

Vegetarian Sausage Rice

2 cups chopped green bell peppers
1 can (15½ ounces) dark kidney beans, drained and rinsed
1 can (14½ ounces) diced tomatoes with green bell peppers and
    onions, undrained
1 cup chopped onion
1 cup sliced celery
1 cup water, divided
¾ cup uncooked long-grain white rice
1¼ teaspoons salt
1 teaspoon hot pepper sauce
½ teaspoon dried thyme leaves
½ teaspoon red pepper flakes
3 bay leaves
1 package (8 ounces) vegetable protein breakfast patties, thawed
2 tablespoons extra virgin olive oil
½ cup chopped fresh parsley
    Additional hot pepper sauce (optional)

1. Combine bell peppers, beans, tomatoes with juice, onion, celery, ½ cup water, rice, salt, pepper sauce, thyme, pepper flakes and bay leaves in slow cooker. Cover; cook on LOW 4 to 5 hours. Remove and dicard bay leaves.

2. Dice breakfast patties. Heat oil in large nonstick skillet over medium-high heat. Add patties; cook 2 minutes or until lightly browned, scraping bottom of skillet occasionally.

3. Place patties in slow cooker. *Do not stir.* Add remaining ½ cup water to skillet; bring to a boil over high heat 1 minute, scraping up bits on bottom of skillet. Add liquid and parsley to slow cooker; stir gently to blend. Serve immediately with additional hot pepper sauce, if desired.   *Makes 8 cups*

Vegetarian Sausage Rice

Vegetarian Lasagna

1 small eggplant, sliced into ½-inch rounds
½ teaspoon salt
2 tablespoons olive oil, divided
1 tablespoon butter
8 ounces mushrooms, sliced
1 small onion, diced
1 can (26 ounces) pasta sauce
1 teaspoon dried basil
1 teaspoon dried oregano
2 cups part-skim ricotta cheese
1½ cups (6 ounces) shredded Monterey Jack cheese
1 cup grated Parmesan cheese, divided
1 package (8 ounces) whole wheat lasagna noodles, cooked and drained
1 medium zucchini, thinly sliced

Slow Cooker Directions

1. Sprinkle eggplant with salt; let sit 10 to 15 minutes. Rinse and pat dry; brush with 1 tablespoon olive oil. Brown on both sides in medium skillet over medium heat. Set aside.

2. Heat remaining 1 tablespoon olive oil and butter in same skillet over medium heat; cook and stir mushrooms and onion until softened. Stir in pasta sauce, basil and oregano. Set aside.

3. Combine ricotta cheese, Monterey Jack cheese and ½ cup Parmesan cheese in medium bowl. Set aside.

4. Spread ⅓ sauce mixture in bottom of slow cooker. Layer with ⅓ lasagna noodles, ½ eggplant, ½ cheese mixture. Repeat layers once. For last layer, use remaining ⅓ of lasagna noodles, zuchinni, remaining ⅓ of sauce mixture and top with remaining ½ cup Parmesan.

5. Cover; cook on LOW 6 hours. Let sit 15 to 20 minutes before serving.

Makes 4 to 6 servings

Vegetarian Lasagna

Meatless Sloppy Joes

2 cups thinly sliced onions
2 cups chopped green bell peppers
1 can (about 15 ounces) kidney beans, drained and mashed
1 can (8 ounces) tomato sauce
2 tablespoons ketchup
1 tablespoon mustard
2 cloves garlic, finely chopped
1 teaspoon chili powder
  Cider vinegar (optional)
2 sandwich rolls, halved

Slow Cooker Directions
Combine all ingredients except sandwich rolls in slow cooker. Cover; cook on LOW 5 to 5½ hours or until vegetables are tender. Season to taste with cider vinegar, if desired. Serve on roll halves. *Makes 4 servings*

Chunky Vegetable Chili

1 medium onion, chopped
2 ribs celery, diced
1 carrot, diced
3 cloves garlic, minced
2 cans (about 15 ounces each) Great Northern beans, rinsed and
    drained
1 cup water
1 cup frozen corn
1 can (6 ounces) tomato paste
1 can (4 ounces) diced mild green chilies, undrained
1 tablespoon chili powder
2 teaspoons dried oregano leaves
1 teaspoon salt

Slow Cooker Directions
Combine all ingredients in slow cooker. Cover; cook on LOW 5½ to 6 hours or until vegetables are tender. *Makes 6 servings*

Bean and Vegetable Burritos

    2 tablespoons chili powder
    2 teaspoons dried oregano leaves
1½ teaspoons ground cumin
    1 large sweet potato, peeled and diced
    1 can black beans or pinto beans, rinsed and drained
    4 cloves garlic, minced
    1 medium onion, halved and thinly sliced
    1 jalapeño pepper,* seeded and minced
    1 green bell pepper, chopped
    1 cup frozen corn, thawed and drained
    3 tablespoons lime juice
    1 tablespoon chopped fresh cilantro
    ¾ cup (3 ounces) shredded Monterey Jack cheese
    4 (10-inch) flour tortillas
      Sour cream (optional)

Jalapeño peppers can sting and irritate the skin; wear rubber gloves when handling peppers and do not touch eyes. Wash hands after handling.

Slow Cooker Directions

1. Combine chili powder, oregano and cumin in small bowl. Set aside.

2. Layer ingredients in slow cooker in the following order: sweet potato, beans, half of chili powder mixture, garlic, onion, jalapeño pepper, bell pepper, remaining half of chili powder mixture and corn. Cover; cook on LOW 5 hours or until sweet potato is tender. Stir in lime juice and cilantro.

3. Preheat oven to 350°F. Spoon 2 tablespoons cheese in center of each tortilla. Top with 1 cup filling. Fold all 4 sides to enclose filling. Place burritos seam side down on baking sheet. Cover with foil and bake 20 to 30 minutes or until heated through. Serve with sour cream, if desired.

Broccoli & Cheese Strata

2 cups chopped broccoli florets
4 slices firm white bread, ½ inch thick
4 teaspoons butter
1½ cups (6 ounces) shredded Cheddar cheese
1½ cups low-fat (1%) milk
3 eggs
½ teaspoon salt
½ teaspoon hot pepper sauce
⅛ teaspoon black pepper

Slow Cooker Directions
1. Cook broccoli in boiling water 10 minutes or until tender. Drain. Spread one side of each bread slice with 1 teaspoon butter. Arrange 2 slices bread, buttered sides up, in greased 1-quart casserole that will fit in slow cooker. Layer cheese, broccoli and remaining 2 bread slices, buttered sides down.

2. Beat milk, eggs, salt, pepper sauce and black pepper in medium bowl. Gradually pour over bread.

3. Place small wire rack in 5-quart slow cooker. Pour in 1 cup water. Place casserole on rack. Cover; cook on HIGH 3 hours.   *Makes 4 servings*

Pesto Rice and Beans

1 can (15 ounces) Great Northern beans, rinsed and drained
1 can (14 ounces) chicken broth
¾ cup uncooked long-grain white rice
1½ cups frozen cut green beans, thawed and drained
½ cup prepared pesto
Grated Parmesan cheese (optional)

Slow Cooker Directions
Combine Great Northern beans, chicken broth and rice in slow cooker. Cover; cook on LOW 2 hours. Stir in green beans; cover and cook 1 hour or until rice and beans are tender. Turn off slow cooker and remove insert to heatproof surface. Stir in pesto and Parmesan cheese, if desired. Let stand, covered, 5 minutes or until cheese is melted. Serve immediately.
Makes 8 servings

Broccoli & Cheese Strata

Slow Cooker Veggie Stew

  1 tablespoon vegetable oil
⅔ cup carrot slices
½ cup diced onion
  2 cloves garlic, chopped
  2 cans (14 ounces each) fat-free vegetable broth
1½ cups chopped green cabbage
  ½ cup cut green beans
  ½ cup diced zucchini
  1 tablespoon tomato paste
  ½ teaspoon dried basil leaves
  ½ teaspoon dried oregano leaves
  ¼ teaspoon salt

Slow Cooker Directions

1. Heat oil in medium skillet over medium-high heat. Add carrot, onion and garlic. Cook and stir until tender.

2. Place carrot mixture and remaining ingredients in slow cooker; stir to combine. Cover; cook on LOW 8 to 10 hours or on HIGH 4 to 5 hours.

Makes 4 to 6 servings

❧ Tip ❧

Do not use the slow cooker to reheat leftover foods. Transfer cooled leftover food to a resealable plastic food storage bag or plastic storage container with a tight-fitting lid and refrigerate. Use a microwave oven, the range-top or oven for reheating.

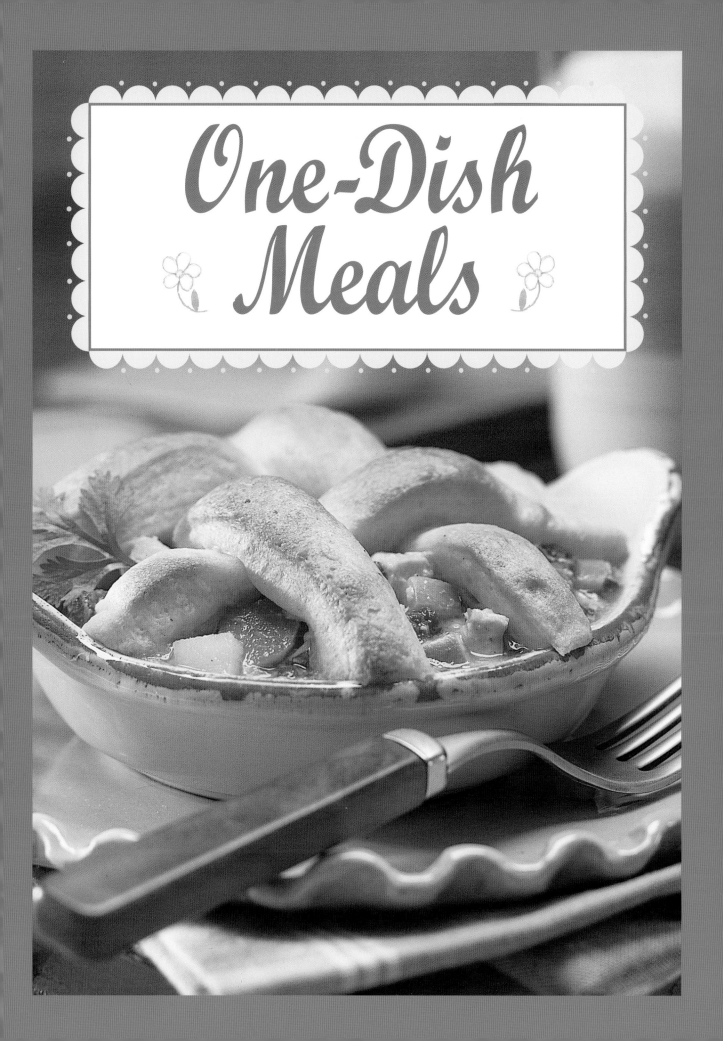

One-Dish Meals

One-Dish Meals

p. 164

p. 182

Steaming Stews
162

Hearty Chilis
182

International Fare
202

Weeknight Meals
222

p. 204

p. 222

Steaming Stews

Italian Vegetable Stew

1 teaspoon olive oil
2 medium zucchini, halved lengthwise and thinly sliced
1 medium eggplant, chopped
1 large onion, thinly sliced
⅛ teaspoon ground black pepper
1 jar (1 pound 10 ounces) RAGÚ® Light Pasta Sauce
3 tablespoons grated Parmesan cheese
1 box (10 ounces) couscous

1. In 12-inch nonstick skillet, heat olive oil over medium heat and cook zucchini, eggplant, onion and pepper, stirring occasionally, 15 minutes or until vegetables are golden.

2. Stir in Ragú Pasta Sauce and cheese. Bring to a boil over high heat. Reduce heat to low and simmer covered 10 minutes.

3. Meanwhile, prepare couscous according to package directions. Serve vegetable mixture over hot couscous. *Makes 4 servings*

Prep Time: 10 minutes
Cook Time: 25 minutes

Italian Vegetable Stew

Hearty Vegetable Gumbo

  Nonstick cooking spray
½ cup chopped onion
½ cup chopped green bell pepper
¼ cup chopped celery
 2 cloves garlic, minced
 2 cans (about 14 ounces each) no-salt-added stewed tomatoes,
    undrained
 2 cups no-salt-added tomato juice
 1 can (15 ounces) red beans, rinsed and drained
 1 tablespoon fresh chopped fresh parsley
¼ teaspoon dried oregano leaves
¼ teaspoon hot pepper sauce
 2 bay leaves
1½ cups quick-cooking brown rice
 1 package (10 ounces) frozen chopped okra, thawed

1. Spray 4-quart Dutch oven with cooking spray; heat over medium heat
until hot. Add onion, bell pepper, celery and garlic. Cook and stir 3 minutes
or until crisp-tender.

2. Add stewed tomatoes with juice, tomato juice, beans, parsley, oregano,
pepper sauce and bay leaves. Bring to a boil over high heat. Add rice. Cover;
reduce heat to medium-low. Simmer 15 minutes or until rice is tender.

3. Add okra; cook, covered, 5 minutes more or until okra is tender. Remove
and discard bay leaves.   *Makes 4 (2-cup) servings*

Hearty Vegetable Gumbo

Salmon, Corn & Barley Chowder

1 teaspoon canola oil
¼ cup chopped onion
1 clove garlic, minced
2½ cups fat-free reduced-sodium chicken broth
¼ cup quick-cooking barley
1 tablespoon water
1 tablespoon all-purpose flour
1 can (4 ounces) salmon, drained
1 cup frozen corn, thawed
⅓ cup reduced-fat (2%) milk
½ teaspoon chili powder
¼ teaspoon ground cumin
¼ teaspoon dried oregano leaves
⅛ teaspoon salt
1 tablespoon minced fresh cilantro
⅛ teaspoon black pepper
Lime wedges (optional)

1. Heat oil in medium saucepan over medium heat until hot. Add onion and garlic. Cook and stir 1 to 2 minutes or until onion is tender.

2. Add broth and bring to a boil. Stir in barley. Cover; reduce heat to low. Simmer 10 minutes or until barley is tender.

3. Stir water slowly into flour in cup until smooth. Remove and discard bones and skin from salmon; flake salmon into bite-size pieces.

4. Add salmon, corn and milk to saucepan; stir until blended. Stir in flour mixture, then chili powder, cumin, oregano and salt. Simmer gently 2 to 3 minutes or until slightly thickened. Stir in cilantro and pepper. Serve with lime wedges, if desired. *Makes 2 (2¼-cup) servings*

Salmon, Corn & Barley Chowder

Ranch Clam Chowder

3 cans (6½ ounces each) chopped clams
6 slices bacon, chopped*
¼ cup finely chopped onion
¼ cup all-purpose flour
2½ cups milk
1 packet (1 ounce) HIDDEN VALLEY® The Original Ranch® Salad
    Dressing & Seasoning Mix
2 cups frozen cubed O'Brien potatoes
2 cups frozen corn kernels
⅛ teaspoon dried thyme (optional)

*Bacon pieces can be used.

Drain clams, reserving juice (about 1⅓ cups); set aside. Cook bacon until crisp in a large pot or Dutch oven; remove with slotted spoon, reserving ¼ cup drippings.** Set aside bacon pieces. Heat bacon drippings over medium heat in same pot. Add onion; sauté 3 minutes. Sprinkle with flour; cook and stir 1 minute longer. Gradually whisk in reserved clam juice and milk, stirring until smooth. Whisk in salad dressing & seasoning mix until blended. Stir in potatoes, corn and thyme, if desired. Bring mixture just to a boil; reduce heat and simmer 10 minutes, stirring occasionally. Stir in clams; heat through. Sprinkle bacon on each serving.

Makes 4 to 6 servings

**You may substitute ¼ cup butter for the bacon drippings.

Cheeseburger Macaroni Stew

1 pound ground beef
1 can (28 ounces) crushed tomatoes in puree
1½ cups uncooked elbow macaroni
2 tablespoons *French's*® Worcestershire Sauce
1 cup shredded Cheddar cheese
1½ cups *French's*® French Fried Onions

1. Cook meat in large nonstick skillet over medium-high heat until browned and no longer pink; drain.

2. Add tomatoes, macaroni and *1½ cups water*. Bring to boiling. Boil, partially covered, 10 minutes until macaroni is tender. Stir in Worcestershire.

3. Sprinkle with cheese and French Fried Onions.   *Makes 6 servings*

Tip: For a Southwestern flavor, add 2 tablespoons chili powder to ground beef and substitute 2 tablespoons *Frank's*® RedHot Sauce for the Worcestershire.

Prep Time: 5 minutes
Cook Time: 15 minutes

Chicken & White Bean Stew

> **1 tablespoon olive oil**
> **2 medium carrots, sliced (about 2 cups)**
> **1 medium onion, thinly sliced**
> **2 cloves garlic, finely chopped**
> **1 tablespoon balsamic vinegar**
> **1 pound boneless, skinless chicken breast halves or thighs, cut into chunks**
> **1 jar (1 pound 10 ounces) RAGÚ® Old World Style® Pasta Sauce**
> **2 cans (15 ounces each) cannellini or white kidney beans, rinsed and drained**
> **Pinch crushed red pepper flakes (optional)**

In 12-inch skillet, heat olive oil over medium heat and cook carrots, onion and garlic, stirring occasionally, 5 minutes or until vegetables are tender. Stir in vinegar and cook 1 minute. Remove vegetables; set aside.

In same skillet, thoroughly brown chicken over medium-high heat. Return vegetables to skillet. Stir in Ragú Old World Style Pasta Sauce, beans and red pepper flakes. Bring to a boil over high heat. Reduce heat to medium and simmer covered, stirring occasionally, 15 minutes or until chicken is thoroughly cooked. Garnish, if desired, with fresh parsley and serve with toasted Italian bread.   *Makes 6 servings*

Basil Pork and Green Bean Stew

  1 package (9 ounces) frozen cut green beans
3½ cups peeled red potatoes cut into ½-inch cubes
  1 pound trimmed pork tenderloin, cut into 1-inch cubes
  1 cup no-sugar-added prepared meatless spaghetti sauce
  ½ teaspoon salt
  1 tablespoon chopped fresh basil *or* 1 teaspoon dried basil leaves
  ¼ cup grated Parmesan cheese

Microwave Directions

1. Place beans in 10- to 12-inch microwavable casserole. Microwave, covered, at HIGH 2 minutes. Drain in colander.

2. Using same dish, microwave potatoes, covered, at HIGH 3 minutes. Stir in pork, beans, spaghetti sauce and salt. Microwave at HIGH 10 minutes, stirring halfway through. Stir in basil. Microwave 5 to 7 minutes or until potatoes are tender and meat is no longer pink in center. Serve with cheese.

Makes 6 servings

French Country Chicken Stew

  ¼ pound sliced bacon, diced
  4 boneless, skinless chicken breast halves, cut into 1-inch pieces
  1 medium onion, chopped
  2 cloves garlic, minced
  1 teaspoon dried thyme leaves, crushed
  1 can (14½ ounces) DEL MONTE® Cut Green Beans, drained
  1 can (15 ounces) kidney beans, drained
  1 can (14½ ounces) DEL MONTE Stewed Tomatoes - Original Recipe
    Salt and pepper to taste

Cook and stir bacon in large skillet over medium-high heat until almost crisp. Add chicken, onion, garlic and thyme. Cook and stir until onion and garlic are soft, about 5 minutes. Pour off drippings. Add remaining ingredients; bring to a boil over high heat. Reduce heat to low. Simmer, uncovered, 10 minutes.

Makes 4 servings

Basil Pork and
Green Bean Stew

Easy Vegetable Beef Stew

1 pound beef for stew, cut into 1-inch pieces
1 can (14½ ounces) diced tomatoes, undrained
1 medium onion, cut into 8 wedges
4 carrots, cut into 1-inch pieces
1 green or red bell pepper, diced
1 rib celery, sliced
1 teaspoon Italian seasoning
½ teaspoon salt
½ teaspoon black pepper
1 tablespoon vegetable oil
1 package (8 ounces) sliced mushrooms

1. Combine beef pieces, tomatoes with juice and onion in Dutch oven. Cover tightly; bake at 325°F 1 hour.

2. Add carrots, bell pepper, celery, Italian seasoning, salt and black pepper to beef mixture; stir. Cover; bake an additional 45 minutes or until beef and carrots are tender.

3. Heat oil in large skillet over medium heat. Add mushrooms; cook and stir 10 minutes or until lightly browned and tender. Stir mushrooms into beef stew. Adjust seasonings to taste. *Makes 4 servings*

Tip

Two unpeeled medium red potatoes, cut into 2-inch pieces, can be added with carrots.

Vegetable Stew Medley

2 tablespoons CRISCO® Oil*
4 medium onions, thinly sliced and separated into rings
3 medium green bell peppers, cut into strips
2 cloves garlic, minced
4 medium zucchini, cut into ½-inch pieces
1 medium eggplant, cut into ½-inch pieces (about 1 pound)
1 can (14½ ounces) no-salt-added whole tomatoes, drained and
    chopped, *or* 4 or 5 fresh tomatoes, peeled and quartered
1 teaspoon dried dill weed
¾ teaspoon dried basil leaves
½ teaspoon dried oregano leaves
½ teaspoon black pepper
¼ teaspoon salt
1 package (9 ounces) frozen peas
¼ cup lemon juice
2 tablespoons chopped fresh parsley *or* 2 teaspoons dried parsley

Use your favorite Crisco Oil product.

1. Heat oil in Dutch oven (non-reactive or non-cast iron) on medium heat. Add onions, bell peppers and garlic. Cook and stir until tender.

2. Add zucchini and eggplant. Cook 5 minutes, stirring occasionally. Stir in tomatoes, dill weed, basil, oregano, black pepper and salt. Reduce heat to low. Cover. Simmer 20 minutes, stirring occasionally.

3. Stir in peas. Simmer 3 to 5 minutes or until peas are thawed and heated, stirring occasionally. Stir in lemon juice. Serve hot or chilled sprinkled with parsley.   *Makes 12 servings*

Hearty Rustic Stew

4 slices thick smoked bacon, diced
3 tablespoons all-purpose flour
½ teaspoon salt
½ teaspoon freshly ground black pepper
1 package JENNIE-O TURKEY STORE® Boneless Breast
   Tenderloins, cut into 1-inch chunks
2 teaspoons bottled or fresh minced garlic
2 cans (13¾ ounces) beef or chicken broth
⅓ cup red wine (optional)
1¼ pounds small red potatoes, halved
8 ounces baby carrots
1 cup thickly sliced celery
4 ounces shallots or small boiling onions, peeled
2 teaspoons herbes de Provence or dried thyme
1 tablespoon butter or margarine
8 ounces cremini, button or small portobello mushrooms, halved

Cook bacon in Dutch oven over medium heat until crisp, stirring
occasionally. Transfer with slotted spoon to medium bowl; set aside.
Meanwhile, in plastic or paper bag combine flour, salt and pepper. Add half
of turkey, shaking to coat. Transfer mixture to drippings in Dutch oven;
cook 5 minutes, stirring occasionally. Transfer to bowl with bacon. Repeat
with remaining turkey; transfer to bowl. Add garlic to Dutch oven; cook
1 minute. Add broth and wine, if desired; bring to a boil, scraping up
browned bits on bottom of Dutch oven. Stir in potatoes, carrots, celery,
shallots and herbes de Provence; return to a boil. Reduce heat; cover and
simmer 20 to 25 minutes or until vegetables are almost tender. Meanwhile,
melt butter in skillet over medium-high heat. Add mushrooms; cook
5 minutes, stirring occasionally. Stir into stew along with reserved turkey
and bacon mixture. Return to simmer; simmer uncovered 10 minutes or
until turkey is no longer pink in center and stew has thickened slightly.

Makes 6 servings

Chicken and Dumplings Stew

2 cans (about 14 ounces each) fat-free reduced-sodium chicken broth
1 pound boneless skinless chicken breasts, cut into bite-size pieces
1 cup diagonally sliced carrots
¾ cup diagonally sliced celery
1 medium onion, halved and cut into small wedges
3 small new potatoes, unpeeled and cut into cubes
½ teaspoon dried rosemary
½ teaspoon black pepper
1 can (14½ ounces) diced tomatoes, drained *or* 1½ cups diced fresh tomatoes
3 tablespoons all-purpose flour blended with ⅓ cup water

DUMPLINGS
¾ cup all-purpose flour
1 teaspoon baking powder
¼ teaspoon onion powder
¼ teaspoon salt
1 to 2 tablespoons finely chopped fresh parsley
¼ cup cholesterol-free egg substitute
¼ cup low-fat (1%) milk
1 tablespoon vegetable oil

1. Bring broth to a boil in Dutch oven; add chicken. Cover; simmer 3 minutes. Add carrots, celery, onion, potatoes, rosemary and pepper. Cover; simmer 10 minutes. Reduce heat; stir in tomatoes and dissolved flour. Cook and stir until broth thickens.

2. Combine ¾ cup flour, baking powder, onion powder and salt in medium bowl; blend in parsley. Combine egg substitute, milk and oil in small bowl; stir into flour mixture just until dry ingredients are moistened.

3. Return broth mixture to a boil. Drop 8 tablespoons of dumpling batter into broth; cover tightly. Reduce heat; simmer 18 to 20 minutes. Do not lift lid. Dumplings are done when toothpick inserted into centers comes out clean.

Makes 4 servings

*Chicken and
Dumplings Stew*

Savory Bean Stew

1 tablespoon olive or vegetable oil
1 cup frozen vegetable blend (onions, celery, red and green bell
    peppers)
1 can (15½ ounces) chick-peas (garbanzo beans), rinsed and drained
1 can (15 ounces) pinto beans, rinsed and drained
1 can (15 ounces) black beans, rinsed and drained
1 can (14½ ounces) diced tomatoes with roasted garlic, undrained
¾ teaspoon dried thyme leaves
¾ teaspoon dried sage leaves
½ to ¾ teaspoon dried oregano leaves
¾ cup vegetable broth or chicken broth, divided
1 tablespoon all-purpose flour
    Salt and black pepper

Polenta
 3 cups water
¾ cup yellow cornmeal
¾ teaspoon salt

1. Heat oil in large saucepan over medium heat until hot. Add vegetable
blend; cook and stir 5 minutes. Stir in beans, tomatoes with juice and herbs.
Mix ½ cup vegetable broth and flour. Stir into bean mixture; bring to a boil.
Boil, stirring constantly, 1 minute. Reduce heat to low; simmer, covered,
10 minutes. Add remaining ¼ cup broth to stew; season to taste with salt
and black pepper.

2. While stew is simmering, prepare Polenta. Bring 3 cups water to a boil.
Reduce heat to medium; gradually stir in cornmeal and salt. Cook 5 to
8 minutes or until cornmeal thickens and holds its shape, but is still soft.
Season to taste with black pepper. Spread Polenta over plate and top with
stew. *Makes 6 (1-cup) servings*

Tip: For a special touch, stir browned smoked sausages, cut into 1-inch
pieces, into the stew for 10 minutes of simmering.

Prep and Cook Time: 30 minutes

Savory Bean Stew

Beef and Parsnip Stew

4½ cups Beef Stock (recipe follows) or beef broth
1¼ pounds beef stew meat, cut into ¾-inch cubes
½ cup all-purpose flour
2 tablespoons vegetable oil
½ cup dry red wine
1 teaspoon salt
½ teaspoon dried Italian seasoning
⅛ teaspoon black pepper
8 ounces peeled baby carrots
2 parsnips, peeled and cut into ½-inch slices
¾ cup sugar snap peas

1. Prepare Beef Stock. Toss beef in flour to coat. Heat oil in large saucepan over medium-high heat. Add beef and remaining flour; brown, stirring frequently.

2. Stir in Beef Stock, wine, salt, Italian seasoning and pepper. Bring to a boil over high heat. Reduce heat to medium-low; simmer, uncovered, 1 hour.

3. Add carrots. Cook 15 minutes. Add parsnips. Simmer 8 minutes or until vegetables and meat are tender.

4. Stir in peas. Cook and stir over medium heat until heated through.

Makes 5 servings

Beef Stock

4 pounds meaty beef bones
2 large onions, cut into wedges
2 large carrots, halved
4 ribs celery, halved
3½ quarts cold water, divided
8 sprigs fresh parsley
2 bay leaves
1 teaspoon dried thyme leaves
6 black peppercorns
3 whole cloves

1. Preheat oven to 450°F. Rinse bones in cold water. Place bones in large roasting pan; roast in oven 30 minutes, turning once.

2. Arrange onions, carrots and celery over bones. Roast 30 minutes more.*

3. Transfer bones and vegetables to stockpot or 5-quart Dutch oven. Skim and discard fat from roasting pan.

4. To deglaze roasting pan, add 2 cups water to pan. Cook over medium-high heat, scraping up brown bits and stirring constantly 2 to 3 minutes or until mixture has reduced by about half. Transfer mixture to stockpot.

5. Add remaining 3 quarts water, parsley, bay leaves, thyme, peppercorns and cloves to stockpot. Bring to a boil over high heat. Reduce heat to medium-low; simmer, uncovered, 3 to 4 hours, skimming foam off top occasionally.

6. Remove stock from heat; cool slightly. Remove large bones. Strain stock through large sieve or colander lined with several layers of damp cheesecloth set over large bowl; discard bones and vegetables.

7. Use immediately or refrigerate stock in tightly covered container up to 2 days or freeze stock in storage containers for several months.

Makes about 1½ quarts stock

For added zip, spread 3 ounces tomato paste over bones at this point. Roast an additional 15 minutes. Proceed as directed in step 3.

 *Tip*

Before freezing, refrigerate the stock until the fat rises to the surface; skim the fat.

Baked Black Bean Chili

1½ pounds 90% lean ground beef
¼ cup chopped sweet onion
¼ cup chopped green bell pepper
1 can (about 15 ounces) black beans, rinsed and drained
1 can (14½ ounces) diced tomatoes with green chilies
1 can (about 14 ounces) beef broth
1 can (8 ounces) tomato sauce
5 tablespoons chili powder
1 tablespoon sugar
1 tablespoon ground cumin
1 teaspoon dried minced onion
⅛ teaspoon garlic powder
⅛ teaspoon ground ginger
2 cups (8 ounces) Mexican-blend shredded cheese

1. Preheat oven to 350°F. Cook and stir beef, onion and bell pepper in large skillet over medium-high heat until meat is no longer pink. Drain and transfer to 4-quart casserole.

2. Add remaining ingredients, except cheese; stir until well blended. Cover and bake 30 minutes, stirring every 10 minutes or so. Uncover, top with cheese, and return to oven about 5 minutes or until cheese melts.

Makes 6 to 8 servings

Baked Black Bean Chili

Rice and Chick-Pea Chili

⅔ cup UNCLE BEN'S® ORIGINAL CONVERTED® Brand Rice
1 can (15 ounces) chick-peas, undrained
1 can (15 ounces) diced tomatoes, undrained
1 can (8 ounces) diced green chilies
1 cup frozen corn
¼ cup chopped fresh cilantro
1 tablespoon taco seasoning
½ cup (2 ounces) shredded reduced-fat Cheddar cheese

1. In medium saucepan, bring 1¾ cups water and rice to a boil. Cover; reduce heat and simmer 15 minutes.

2. Add remaining ingredients except cheese. Cook over low heat 10 minutes. Serve in bowls sprinkled with cheese. *Makes 4 servings*

Serving Suggestion: To round out the meal, serve this hearty chili with corn bread and fresh fruit.

White Chicken Chili

1 to 2 tablespoons canola oil
1 onion, chopped (about 1 cup)
1 package (about 1¼ pounds) PERDUE® Fresh Ground Chicken, Turkey or Turkey Breast Meat
1 package (about 1¾ ounces) chili seasoning mix
1 can (14½ ounces) reduced-sodium chicken broth
1 can (15 ounces) cannellini or white kidney beans, drained and rinsed

In Dutch oven over medium-high heat, heat oil. Add onions; sauté 2 to 3 minutes, until softened and translucent. Add ground chicken; sauté 5 to 7 minutes, until no longer pink. Add chili mix and stir to combine. Add chicken broth and beans; bring to a boil. Reduce heat to medium-low; simmer 5 to 10 minutes, until all flavors are blended. *Makes 4 servings*

Prep Time: 10 minutes
Cook Time: 10 to 20 minutes

Rice and Chick-Pea Chili

Spicy Vegetable Chili

½ cup uncooked wheat berries
1 large onion, chopped
½ green bell pepper, chopped
½ yellow or red bell pepper, chopped
2 ribs celery, sliced
3 cloves garlic, minced
1 can (14½ ounces) chopped tomatoes
1 can (15 ounces) red kidney beans, rinsed and drained
1 can (15 ounces) chick-peas (garbanzo beans), rinsed and drained
¾ cup raisins
½ cup water
1 tablespoon chili seasoning blend or chili powder
1 teaspoon dried oregano leaves
1 tablespoon chopped fresh parsley
1½ teaspoons hot pepper sauce

1. Place wheat berries in small saucepan and cover with 2 cups water; let soak overnight. Bring to a boil over high heat. Reduce heat to low; cover and cook 45 minutes to 1 hour or until wheat berries are tender. Drain; set aside.

2. Spray large skillet or saucepan with nonstick cooking spray; heat over medium heat. Add onion; cover and cook 5 minutes. Add bell peppers, celery and garlic; cover and cook 5 minutes, stirring occasionally.

3. Add tomatoes, kidney beans, chick-peas, raisins, ½ cup water, chili seasoning, oregano and wheat berries to skillet; mix well. Bring to a boil over high heat. Reduce heat to low; simmer 25 to 30 minutes, stirring occasionally. Just before serving, stir in parsley and hot pepper sauce. Garnish, if desired.

Makes 4 servings

Spicy Vegetable Chili

Southwest Chicken Chili

⅓ cup CRISCO® Corn Oil
1 large onion, chopped
2 garlic cloves, minced
1 red bell pepper, diced
3 teaspoons chili powder
2 teaspoons cumin
2 cans (15 ounces each) cannellini beans, rinsed and drained
2 cans (14 ounces each) chicken broth
2 cans (4 ounces each) chopped mild green chilies
6 cups cooked chicken, cut into ½-inch pieces
   Hot sauce to taste
   Salt and pepper to taste

Garnish (as desired)
   Shredded Monterey Jack cheese
   Sour cream
   Chopped fresh cilantro
   Tortilla chips

Heat CRISCO® Corn Oil in a large heavy pot over medium heat.

Add onion and garlic. Cook until softened, about 3 minutes. Add red bell pepper and sauté until just softened, about 1 minute. Add spices and cook until aromatic, about 1 minute more.

Add, beans, broth, green chilies and chicken. Bring mixture to a boil and then simmer, stirring occasionally, 15 to 20 minutes.

Season to taste with hot sauce, salt and pepper.

Ladle into bowls and garnish with shredded Monterey Jack cheese, sour cream and cilantro as desired. *Makes 6 to 8 servings*

Chicken and Black Bean Chili

1 medium onion, chopped
1 tablespoon vegetable oil
3½ cups shredded, cooked chicken
2 cans (14½ ounces each) diced tomatoes, with juice
1 can (15 ounces) black beans, rinsed and drained
1 can (4 ounces) diced green chiles
½ cup water
½ teaspoon LAWRY'S® Garlic Powder With Parsley
1 package (1.48 ounces) LAWRY'S® Spices & Seasonings for Chili
½ teaspoon hot pepper sauce (optional)
1 tablespoon chopped cilantro

In large deep skillet, heat oil over medium high and cook onion. Add remaining ingredients except cilantro. Bring to a boil; reduce heat to low and cook, uncovered for 20 minutes, stirring occasionally. Stir in cilantro.

Makes 5 ½ cups

Variation: Instead of shredded chicken, try 1½ pounds ground turkey, browned.

Prep. Time: 10 minutes
Cook Time: 23 minutes

Tip

Serve with sour cream and tortilla chips. Diced avocados make a great garnish, too.

Country Sausage Chili

2 pounds bulk spicy beef sausage
2 green bell peppers, seeded and chopped
2 cups chopped onion
1 tablespoon chopped garlic
1 tablespoon brown mustard seeds
4 tablespoons ground chili powder
1 bay leaf
2 teaspoons red pepper flakes
¼ cup molasses
2 cans (28 ounces each) crushed tomatoes
2 cans (4 ounces each) diced green chilies
Hot pepper sauce to taste

1. Brown beef sausage in a large Dutch oven over medium heat. Drain excess fat, leaving 2 tablespoons fat in pot with browned sausage. Break sausage into chunks with wooden spoon. Stir in bell peppers, onion and garlic. Cook and stir until onion is translucent, about 5 to 8 minutes.

2. Add mustard seeds, chili powder, bay leaf, red pepper flakes, molasses, crushed tomatoes, diced green chilies and hot sauce. Simmer until thickened, about 1 hour. Remove and discard bay leaf. Serve with biscuits or cornbread, if desired. *Makes 6 to 8 servings*

Country Sausage Chili

Cincinnati 5-Way Chili

12 ounces ground turkey
1 cup chopped onion, divided
3 cloves garlic, minced
1 can (8 ounces) reduced-sodium tomato sauce
¾ cup water
1 to 2 tablespoons chili powder
1 tablespoon unsweetened cocoa powder
1 to 2 teaspoons cider vinegar
1 teaspoon ground cinnamon
½ teaspoon ground allspice
½ teaspoon paprika
⅛ teaspoon ground cloves (optional)
1 bay leaf
　Salt and black pepper
8 ounces hot cooked spaghetti
½ cup (2 ounces) shredded fat-free Cheddar cheese
½ cup canned red kidney beans, rinsed and drained

1. Cook and stir turkey in medium saucepan over medium heat about 5 minutes or until browned and no longer pink. Drain excess fat. Add ½ cup onion and garlic; cook about 5 minutes or until onion is tender.

2. Add tomato sauce, water, chili powder, cocoa, vinegar, cinnamon, allspice, paprika, cloves and bay leaf; bring to a boil. Reduce heat and simmer, covered, 15 minutes, stirring occasionally. If thicker consistency is desired, simmer uncovered, about 5 minutes more. Discard bay leaf; season to taste with salt and pepper.

3. Spoon spaghetti into bowls; spoon sauce over and sprinkle with remaining ½ cup onion, cheese and beans.　　*Makes 4 main-dish servings*

Cincinnati 5-Way Chili

Winter White Chili

½ pound boneless pork loin *or* 2 boneless pork chops, cut into
    ½-inch cubes
½ cup chopped onion
1 teaspoon vegetable oil
1 (16-ounce) can navy beans, drained
1 (16-ounce) can chick-peas, drained
1 (16-ounce) can white kernel corn, drained
1 (14½-ounce) can chicken broth
1 cup cooked wild rice
1 (4-ounce) can diced green chilies, drained
1½ teaspoons ground cumin
¼ teaspoon garlic powder
⅛ teaspoon hot pepper sauce
    Chopped fresh parsley and shredded cheese

In 4-quart saucepan, sauté pork and onion in oil over medium-high heat
until onion is soft and pork is lightly browned, about 5 minutes. Stir in
remaining ingredients except parsley and shredded cheese. Cover and
simmer for 20 minutes. Serve each portion garnished with parsley and
shredded cheese. *Makes 6 servings*

Prep Time: 10 minutes
Cook Time: 25 minutes

Favorite recipe from *National Pork Board*

Santa Fe Turkey Chili

1 tablespoon vegetable oil
1 cup onion, chopped
2 cloves garlic, chopped
1 tablespoon chili powder
1 (16-ounce) can whole tomatoes, undrained and cut-up
1 (15-ounce) can herbed tomato sauce
1 (16-ounce) can red kidney beans, drained
1 cup frozen whole kernel corn
2 cups JENNIE-O TURKEY STORE® Turkey, cooked and cubed
¼ teaspoon or to taste cayenne pepper (optional)

In Dutch oven or large saucepan over medium-high heat, heat oil until hot. Cook onion and garlic until tender. Stir in chili powder. Add tomatoes with juice, beans and corn. Reduce heat to low; cover and simmer 10 minutes, stirring occasionally. Uncover, add turkey and simmer 5 minutes longer. Serve with yogurt, shredded cheese, sliced green onion and warm corn tortillas, if desired.   *Makes 6 servings*

Prep Time: 30 minutes
Cook Time: 30 minutes

195

Chili Verde

½ to ¾ pound boneless lean pork, cut into 1-inch cubes
1 large onion, halved and thinly sliced
½ cup water
6 cloves garlic, chopped or sliced
1 pound fresh tomatillos, husked
1 can (about 14 ounces) chicken broth
1 can (4 ounces) diced mild green chilies
1 teaspoon ground cumin
1½ cups cooked navy or Great Northern beans *or* 1 can (15 ounces)
    Great Northern beans, rinsed and drained
½ cup lightly packed fresh cilantro, chopped
    Sour cream (optional)
    Jalapeño peppers*, sliced (optional)

Jalapeño peppers can sting and irritate the skin; wear rubber gloves when handling peppers and do not touch eyes. Wash hands after handling.

1. Place pork, onion, water, and garlic in large saucepan. Cover; simmer over medium-low heat 30 minutes, stirring occasionally (add more water if necessary). Uncover; boil over medium-high heat until liquid evaporates and meat browns.

2. Stir in tomatillos and broth. Cover; simmer over medium heat 20 minutes or until tomatillos are tender. Pull tomatillos apart with 2 forks. Add chilies and cumin.

3. Cover; simmer over medium-low heat 45 minutes or until meat is tender and pulls apart easily. (Add more water or broth if necessary, to keep liquid at same level.) Add beans; simmer 10 minutes or until heated through. Stir in cilantro. Serve with sour cream and top with jalapeño slices, if desired.

Makes 4 servings

Chili Verde

Beef Chuck Chili

½ cup olive oil
5 pounds beef chuck roast, visible fat removed
3 cups minced onions
2 green bell peppers, seeded and diced
4 poblano chilies, seeded and diced*
2 serrano chilies, seeded and diced*
3 jalapeño chilies, seeded and diced*
2 tablespoons minced garlic
1 can (28 ounces) crushed tomatoes
1 tablespoon ground cumin
¼ cup hot pepper sauce
   Ground black pepper to taste
4 ounces Mexican lager beer (optional)

Chilie peppers can sting and irritate the skin; wear rubber gloves when handling peppers and do not touch eyes. Wash hands after handling.

Slow Cooker Directions

1. In large skillet over medium-high heat, add olive oil; when sizzling, add chuck roast. Sear on both sides and remove beef to slow cooker.

2. Place onions, bell pepper, chilies and garlic in skillet and reduce heat to low. Cook and stir 7 minutes. Scrape contents of skillet into slow cooker. Add crushed tomatoes. Cover slow cooker and cook on LOW 4 to 5 hours. Beef should be fork tender.

3. Use fork to shred beef. Stir in cumin, hot pepper sauce, pepper and beer, if desired. Serve over rice or cornbread. *Makes 8 to 10 servings*

Beef Chuck Chili

Hearty Chili with Black Beans

1 tablespoon vegetable oil
1 pound ground beef chuck
1 can (about 14½ ounces) beef broth
1 large onion, minced
1 green bell pepper, seeded and diced
2 teaspoons chili powder
½ teaspoon ground allspice
¼ teaspoon cinnamon
¼ teaspoon paprika
1 can (15 ounces) black beans, rinsed and drained
1 can (14 ounces) crushed tomatoes in tomato purée
2 teaspoons apple cider vinegar

1. Heat oil in large skillet over medium high heat until hot. Add ground beef, beef broth, onion and bell pepper. Cook and stir, breaking up meat. Cook until beef is no longer pink; drain excess fat.

2. Add chili powder, allspice, cinnamon and paprika. Reduce heat to medium-low; simmer 10 minutes. Add black beans, tomatoes and vinegar; bring to a boil.

3. Reduce heat to low; simmer 20 to 25 minutes or until chili is thickened to desired consistency. Garnish as desired. *Makes 4 servings*

Tip

Garnish this chili with shredded Cheddar cheese, sour cream and sliced green onions, if desired.

*Hearty Chili with
Black Beans*

International Fare

Oriental Chicken & Rice

1 (6.9-ounce) package RICE-A-RONI® Chicken Flavor
2 tablespoons margarine or butter
1 pound boneless, skinless chicken breasts, cut into thin strips
¼ cup teriyaki sauce
½ teaspoon ground ginger
1 (16-ounce) package frozen Oriental-style mixed vegetables

1. In large skillet over medium heat, sauté rice-vermicelli mix with margarine until vermicelli is golden brown.

2. Slowly stir in 2 cups water, chicken, teriyaki sauce, ginger and Special Seasonings; bring to a boil. Reduce heat to low. Cover; simmer 10 minutes.

3. Stir in vegetables. Cover; simmer 5 to 10 minutes or until rice is tender and chicken is no longer pink inside. Let stand 3 minutes.

Makes 4 servings

Variation: Use pork instead of chicken and substitute ¼ cup orange juice for ¼ cup of the water.

Prep Time: 5 minutes
Cook Time: 25 minutes

Oriental Chicken & Rice

Spicy Lasagna Rollers

1½ pounds Italian sausage, casings removed
1 jar (28 ounces) spaghetti sauce, divided
1 can (8 ounces) tomato sauce
½ cup chopped roasted red pepper
¾ teaspoon dried Italian seasoning
½ teaspoon red pepper flakes
1 container (15 ounces) ricotta cheese
1 package (10 ounces) frozen chopped spinach, thawed and
    squeezed dry
2 cups (8 ounces) shredded Italian cheese blend, divided
1 cup (4 ounces) shredded Cheddar cheese, divided
1 egg, lightly beaten
12 lasagna noodles, cooked and drained

1. Preheat oven to 350°F. Spray 13×9-inch baking pan with nonstick cooking spray; set aside.

2. Cook sausage in large skillet over medium heat until browned, stirring to break up meat; drain. Stir in ½ cup spaghetti sauce, tomato sauce, roasted red pepper, Italian seasoning and pepper flakes.

3. Mix ricotta, spinach, 1½ cups Italian cheese blend, ½ cup Cheddar cheese and egg in medium bowl. Spread ¼ cup ricotta mixture over each noodle. Top with ⅓ cup sausage mixture. Tightly roll up each noodle from short end, jelly-roll style. Place rolls, seam sides down, in prepared pan. Pour remaining spaghetti sauce over rolls. Sprinkle with remaining ½ cup Italian cheese blend and ½ cup Cheddar cheese. Cover pan with foil.

4. Bake 30 minutes. Carefully remove foil; bake 15 minutes or until sauce is bubbly. *Makes 6 servings*

Mexi-Tortilla Casserole

1 tablespoon vegetable oil
1 small onion, chopped
1 pound ground pork*
1 can (14½ ounces) diced tomatoes, undrained
1 teaspoon dried oregano
¼ teaspoon salt
¼ teaspoon ground cumin
¼ teaspoon pepper
1½ cups (6 ounces) shredded pepper-Jack or taco-flavored cheese
2 cups tortilla chips
½ cup reduced-fat sour cream
1 can (4 ounces) diced green chilies, drained
2 tablespoons minced cilantro

*For a vegetarian casserole, substitute 1 pound tofu crumbles for the pork.

1. Preheat oven to 350°F.

2. Heat oil in large skillet. Add onion and cook 5 minutes or until tender. Add pork and cook until brown, stirring to separate meat. Pour off fat. Stir in tomatoes with juice, oregano, salt, cumin and pepper. Spoon into 11×7-inch casserole. Sprinkle cheese over casserole; arrange tortilla chips over cheese. Bake 10 to 15 minutes or until cheese melts.

3. Combine sour cream and chilies; mix until well blended. Drop by tablespoonfuls over baked casserole. Sprinkle with cilantro.

Makes 6 servings

Mexi-Tortilla Casserole

Chicken Normandy Style

2 tablespoons butter, divided
3 cups peeled, thinly sliced apples, such as Fuji or Braeburn (about 3 apples)
1 pound ground chicken
¼ cup apple brandy or apple juice
1 can (10¾ ounces) condensed cream of chicken soup, undiluted
¼ cup finely chopped green onions (green part only)
2 teaspoons fresh minced sage *or* ½ teaspoon dried sage leaves
¼ teaspoon black pepper
1 package (12 ounces) egg noodles, cooked and drained

1. Preheat oven to 350°F. Grease 9-inch square casserole dish.

2. Melt 1 tablespoon butter in 12-inch nonstick skillet. Add apple slices; cook and stir over medium heat 7 to 10 minutes or until tender. Remove apple slices from skillet.

3. Add ground chicken to same skillet; cook and stir over medium heat until brown, breaking up with spoon. Stir in apple brandy and cook 2 minutes. Stir in soup, green onions, sage, pepper and apple slices. Simmer 5 minutes.

4. Toss noodles with remaining 1 tablespoon butter. Spoon into prepared casserole. Top with chicken mixture. Bake 15 minutes or until hot.

Makes 4 servings

Note: Ground turkey, ground pork or tofu crumbles can be substituted for chicken, if desired.

Chilaquiles

2 tablespoons vegetable oil
1 medium onion, chopped
1 package (1.0 ounce) LAWRY'S® Taco Spices & Seasonings
1 can (28 ounces) diced tomatoes, in juice
1 can (4 ounces) diced green chiles (optional)
6 ounces tortilla chips
4 cups (16 ounces) shredded Monterey Jack cheese
1 cup sour cream
½ cup (2 ounces) shredded cheddar cheese

In large skillet, heat oil over medium high heat. Add onion and cook until tender. Add Taco Spices & Seasonings, tomatoes and chiles; mix well. Bring to a boil; reduce heat to low and cook, uncovered, 10 minutes, stirring occasionally. Spray 2-quart casserole dish with nonstick cooking spray; arrange ½ of tortilla chips, sauce and Monterey Jack cheese. Repeat layers; top with sour cream. Bake in 350°F oven for 25 minutes. Sprinkle with cheddar cheese and bake 5 minutes longer. Let stand 10 minutes before serving. *Makes 6 to 8 servings*

Meal Idea: Serve with a marinated vegetable salad and fresh fruit.

Prep. Time: 12 to 15 minutes
Cook Time: 45 to 50 minutes

Spanish Skillet Supper

1 tablespoon vegetable oil
1 pound boneless skinless chicken breasts, cut into 1-inch cubes
2 cups hot water
1 package (4.4 ounces) Spanish rice and sauce mix
2 cups BIRDS EYE® frozen Green Peas
  Crushed red pepper flakes

- Heat oil in large skillet over medium-high heat. Add chicken; cook and stir until lightly browned, about 5 minutes.

- Add hot water, rice and sauce mix; bring to boil. Reduce heat to medium-low; simmer, uncovered, 5 minutes.

- Stir in green peas; increase heat to medium-high. Cover and cook 5 minutes or until peas and rice are tender.

- Sprinkle with red pepper flakes.   *Makes about 4 servings*

Prep Time: 5 minutes
Cook Time: 20 minutes

One-Pan Chicken Alfredo

1¼ **pounds skinless, chicken breasts**
 2 **tablespoons CRISCO® Oil***
 2 **cans (14½ ounces each) chicken broth**
 1 **package (8 ounces) uncooked rotini pasta**
1½ **cups baby carrots, sliced into thin rounds**
 1 **tablespoon plus 1½ teaspoons cornstarch**
 1 **package (1.6 ounces) garlic-herb pasta sauce mix**
1½ **cups skim milk**
 1 **package (10 ounces) frozen chopped broccoli, thawed, drained and squeezed dry**
 ⅓ **cup Parmesan cheese**

*Use your favorite Crisco Oil product.

Rinse chicken; pat dry. Cut into ¾-inch pieces. Heat oil in deep nonstick 12-inch skillet or Dutch oven on medium-high heat. Add chicken. Cook and stir for 3 minutes or until no longer pink in center. Stir in broth and rotini. Bring to a boil. Reduce heat to medium. Cover. Simmer 5 minutes. Add carrots. Stir and cover. Cook 4 to 5 minutes longer.

Place cornstarch and pasta sauce mix in small bowl. Whisk in milk until smooth. Add gradually to chicken mixture, stirring constantly. Mix in broccoli. Cook and stir for 3 to 5 minutes or until sauce comes to a boil and is thickened. Remove from heat. Sprinkle with cheese. Cover. Let stand 5 minutes. Serve.   *Makes 6 servings*

Pork & Rice Provençal

4 well-trimmed boneless pork loin chops, ¾-inch thick (about
   1 pound)
1 teaspoon dried basil
½ teaspoon dried thyme
½ teaspoon garlic salt
¼ teaspoon ground black pepper
2 tablespoons margarine or butter, divided
1 (6.8-ounce) package RICE-A-RONI® Beef Flavor
½ cup chopped onion
1 clove garlic, minced
1 (14½-ounce) can seasoned diced tomatoes, undrained
1 (2¼-ounce) can sliced ripe olives, drained *or* ⅓ cup sliced pitted
   kalamata olives

1. Sprinkle pork chops with basil, thyme, garlic salt and pepper; set aside.
In large skillet over medium-high heat, melt 1 tablespoon margarine. Add
pork chops; cook 3 minutes. Reduce heat to medium; turn pork chops over
and cook 3 minutes. Remove from skillet; set aside.

2. In same skillet over medium heat, sauté rice-vermicelli mix, onion and
garlic with remaining 1 tablespoon margarine until vermicelli is golden
brown.

3. Slowly stir in 1¾ cups water, tomatoes and Special Seasonings; bring to a
boil. Cover; reduce heat to low. Simmer 10 minutes.

4. Add pork chops and olives. Cover; simmer 10 minutes or until rice is
tender and pork chops are no longer pink inside.   *Makes 4 servings*

Prep Time: 10 minutes
Cook Time: 40 minutes

Pork & Rice Provençal

Simmered Tuscan Chicken

2 tablespoons olive oil
1 pound boneless, skinless chicken breasts, cut into 1-inch cubes
2 cloves garlic, finely chopped
2 medium potatoes, cut into ½-inch cubes (about 4 cups)
1 medium red bell pepper, cut into large pieces
1 jar (1 pound 10 ounces) RAGÚ® Old World Style® Pasta Sauce
1 teaspoon dried basil leaves, crushed
   Salt and ground black pepper to taste

In 12-inch skillet, heat olive oil over medium-high heat and cook chicken with garlic until chicken is thoroughly cooked. Remove chicken and set aside.

In same skillet, add potatoes and bell pepper. Cook over medium heat, stirring occasionally, 5 minutes. Stir in remaining ingredients. Bring to a boil over high heat. Reduce heat to low and simmer covered, stirring occasionally, 35 minutes or until potatoes are tender. Return chicken to skillet and heat through.   *Makes 6 servings*

Szechwan Beef Lo Mein

1 boneless beef top sirloin steak (about 1 pound)
4 cloves garlic, minced
2 teaspoons minced fresh ginger
¾ teaspoon red pepper flakes, divided
1 tablespoon vegetable oil
1 can (about 14 ounces) vegetable broth
1 cup water
2 tablespoons reduced-sodium soy sauce
1 package (8 ounces) frozen mixed vegetables for stir-fry
1 package (9 ounces) refrigerated angel hair pasta
¼ cup chopped fresh cilantro (optional)

1. Cut steak lengthwise in half, then crosswise into thin slices. Toss steak with garlic, ginger and ½ teaspoon red pepper flakes.

2. Heat oil in large nonstick skillet over medium-high heat. Add half of beef to skillet; stir-fry 2 minutes or until meat is barely pink in center. Remove from skillet; set aside. Repeat with remaining beef.

3. Add vegetable broth, water, soy sauce and remaining ¼ teaspoon red pepper flakes to skillet; bring to a boil over high heat. Add vegetables; return to a boil. Reduce heat to low; simmer, covered, 3 minutes or until vegetables are crisp-tender.

4. Uncover; stir in pasta. Return to a boil over high heat. Reduce heat to medium; simmer, uncovered, 2 minutes, separating pasta with two forks. Return steak and any accumulated juices to skillet; simmer 1 minute or until pasta is tender and steak is hot. Sprinkle with cilantro, if desired.

Makes 4 servings

Szechwan Beef Lo Mein

Italian-Glazed Pork Chops

1 tablespoon olive oil
8 bone-in pork chops
1 medium zucchini, thinly sliced
1 medium red bell pepper, chopped
1 medium onion, thinly sliced
3 cloves garlic, finely chopped
¼ cup dry red wine or beef broth
1 jar (1 pound 10 ounces) RAGÚ® Chunky Gardenstyle Pasta Sauce

1. In 12-inch skillet, heat olive oil over medium-high heat and brown chops. Remove chops and set aside.

2. In same skillet, cook zucchini, red bell pepper, onion and garlic, stirring occasionally, 4 minutes. Stir in wine and Ragú Pasta Sauce.

3. Return chops to skillet, turning to coat with sauce. Simmer covered 15 minutes or until chops are tender and barely pink in the center. Serve, if desired, over hot cooked couscous or rice.   *Makes 8 servings*

Prep Time: 10 minutes
Cook Time: 25 minutes

Italian-Glazed Pork Chop

Salsa Chicken & Rice Skillet

1 (6.9-ounce) package RICE-A-RONI® Chicken Flavor
2 tablespoons margarine or butter
1 pound boneless, skinless chicken breasts, cut into 1-inch pieces
1 cup salsa
1 cup frozen or canned corn, drained
1 cup (4 ounces) shredded Cheddar cheese
1 medium tomato, chopped (optional)

1. In large skillet over medium heat, sauté rice-vermicelli mix with margarine until vermicelli is golden brown.

2. Slowly stir in 2 cups water, chicken, salsa and Special Seasonings. Bring to a boil. Reduce heat to low. Cover; simmer 15 minutes.

3. Stir in corn. Cover; simmer 5 minutes or until rice is tender and chicken is no longer pink inside. Top with cheese and tomato, if desired. Cover; let stand 5 minutes for cheese to melt.   *Makes 4 servings*

Prep Time: 5 minutes
Cook Time: 30 minutes

Salsa Chicken & Rice Skillet

Weeknight Meals

Chicken and Stuffing

½ cup all-purpose flour
¾ teaspoon seasoned salt
¾ teaspoon black pepper
4 to 6 boneless skinless chicken breasts (about 1 to 1½ pounds)
¼ cup (½ stick) butter
2 cans (10¾ ounces each) condensed cream of mushroom soup, undiluted
1 package (12 ounces) seasoned stuffing mix, plus ingredients to prepare mix

Slow Cooker Directions

1. Combine flour, seasoned salt and pepper in large resealable plastic food storage bag. Dredge chicken in flour mixture.

2. Melt butter in large skillet over medium-low heat. Brown chicken on both sides. Place in slow cooker. Pour soup over top.

3. Follow package directions for stuffing, decreasing liquid by half. Add stuffing to slow cooker over chicken. Cover; cook on HIGH 3 to 4 hours.

Makes 4 to 6 servings

Chicken and Stuffing

Creole Shrimp and Rice

    2 tablespoons olive oil
    1 cup uncooked white rice
    1 can (15 ounces) diced tomatoes with garlic, undrained
 1½ cups water
    1 teaspoon Creole or Cajun seasoning blend
    1 pound peeled cooked medium shrimp
    1 package (10 ounces) frozen okra *or* 1½ cups frozen sugar snap
       peas, thawed

1. Heat oil in large skillet over medium heat until hot. Add rice; cook and stir 2 to 3 minutes or until lightly browned.

2. Add tomatoes with juice, water and seasoning blend; bring to a boil. Reduce heat; cover and simmer 15 minutes.

3. Add shrimp and okra. Cook, covered, 3 minutes or until heated through.

Makes 4 servings

Prep and Cook Time: 20 minutes

✎ *Tip* ✎

Okra are oblong green pods. When cooked, it gives off a viscous substance that acts as a great thickener for soups and stews.

Creole Shrimp and Rice

224

Saffron Chicken & Vegetables

2 tablespoons vegetable oil

6 bone-in chicken thighs, skinned

1 bag (16 ounces) frozen mixed vegetables, such as broccoli, red peppers, mushrooms and onions, thawed

1 can (14½ ounces) roasted garlic-flavored chicken broth

1 can (10¾ ounces) condensed cream of chicken soup, undiluted

1 can (10¾ ounces) condensed cream of mushroom soup, undiluted

1 package (about 8 ounces) uncooked saffron yellow rice mix with seasonings

½ cup water

½ teaspoon salt

1 teaspoon paprika (optional)

1. Preheat oven to 350°F. Spray 3-quart casserole with nonstick cooking spray; set aside.

2. Heat oil in large skillet over medium heat. Brown chicken on both sides; drain fat.

3. Meanwhile, combine vegetables, chicken broth, soups, rice mix with seasonings, water and salt in large bowl. Place mixture in prepared casserole. Top with chicken. Sprinkle with paprika, if desired. Cover; bake 1½ hours or until chicken is no longer pink in center.   *Makes 6 servings*

Saffron Chicken & Vegetables

Classic Stuffed Shells

1 jar (1 pound 10 ounces) RAGÚ® Old World Style® Pasta Sauce,
    divided
2 pounds ricotta cheese
2 cups shredded mozzarella cheese (about 8 ounces)
¼ cup grated Parmesan cheese
3 eggs
1 tablespoon finely chopped fresh parsley
⅛ teaspoon ground black pepper
1 box (12 ounces) jumbo shells pasta, cooked and drained

Preheat oven to 350°F. In 13×9-inch baking pan, evenly spread 1 cup Ragú
Old World Style Pasta Sauce; set aside.

In large bowl, combine cheeses, eggs, parsley and black pepper. Fill shells
with cheese mixture, then arrange in baking pan. Evenly top with
remaining sauce. Bake 45 minutes or until sauce is bubbling.

Makes 8 servings

⌘ *Tip* ⌘

*For a change of shape, substitute cooked and drained
cannelloni or manicotti tubes for the jumbo shells. Use a
teaspoon or pastry bag to fill the tubes from end to end,
being careful not to overfill them.*

Classic Stuffed Shells

Classic Turkey Pot Pie

2 cups JENNIE-O TURKEY STORE® Turkey Roast, cooked, cubed
    OR 2 cups JENNIE-O TURKEY STORE® Turkey Breast, cooked,
    cubed
1 package (1 pound) frozen stew vegetables, thawed and drained
1 cup frozen peas, thawed and drained
1 (12 ounces) jar non-fat turkey gravy
1 tablespoon dried parsley
½ teaspoon salt
¼ teaspoon black pepper
1 (9-inch) refrigerated pie crust

Heat oven to 400°F. In bowl, combine stew vegetables, peas, turkey, turkey gravy, parsley, salt and black pepper. Place mixture in deep dish 9-inch pie plate. Place pie crust on top of dish, folding edges under to seal. Flute. Cut several slits in crust. Bake 25 to 30 minutes or until crust is golden brown and mixture is hot and bubbly. Serve immediately. *Makes 4 servings*

Cook Time: 30 minutes

Cajun Chicken

2½ pounds chicken pieces, skinned (breasts, thighs, legs)
  1 tablespoon vegetable oil
  2 cloves garlic, crushed
 ½ teaspoon dried thyme
  1 can (14½ ounces) DEL MONTE® Stewed Tomatoes - Original
    Recipe
  1 red or green pepper, cut into strips
  1 stalk celery, sliced
  1 carrot, thinly sliced

1. Brown chicken in oil in large skillet over medium-high heat, 10 to 15 minutes; drain. Season with salt and pepper, if desired.

2. Stir garlic and thyme into tomatoes; pour over chicken. Add pepper strips, celery and carrot.

3. Bring to boil; cover and simmer 15 minutes or until chicken is no longer pink. Garnish with sliced green onions and serve with hot pepper sauce, if desired.   *Makes 4 to 6 servings*

Prep Time: 8 minutes
Cook Time: 30 minutes

Lemon Garlic Chicken & Rice

   4 boneless, skinless chicken breast halves (about 1 pound)
   ½ teaspoon paprika
   ⅛ teaspoon ground black pepper
   2 tablespoons margarine or butter, divided
   1 (6.9-ounce) package RICE-A-RONI® Chicken & Garlic Flavor
   2 teaspoons lemon juice
   1 medium red and/or green bell pepper, chopped

1. Sprinkle chicken with paprika and black pepper; set aside. In large skillet over medium heat, melt 1 tablespoon margarine. Add chicken; cook 2 minutes on each side. Remove from skillet; set aside.

2. In same skillet over medium heat, sauté rice-vermicelli mix with remaining 1 tablespoon margarine until vermicelli is golden brown.

3. Slowly stir in 2 cups water, lemon juice and Special Seasonings; bring to a boil. Place chicken over rice. Reduce heat to low. Cover; simmer 15 minutes.

4. Stir in bell pepper. Cover; cook 5 minutes or until rice is tender and chicken is no longer pink inside.   *Makes 4 servings*

Tip: No lemon juice in the house? Try orange juice.

Prep Time: 5 minutes
Cook Time: 30 minutes

231

Curried Chicken Pot Pies

1 tablespoon canola oil
¾ cup chopped peeled Granny Smith apple
⅓ cup thinly sliced carrot
¼ cup chopped onion
1 clove garlic, minced
1 tablespoon flour
½ teaspoon curry powder
⅛ teaspoon salt
⅛ teaspoon black pepper
    Pinch ground cloves
¾ cup water
1 cup chopped cooked chicken breast
½ cup no-salt-added diced tomatoes, undrained
2 tablespoons minced fresh cilantro
4 refrigerated soft breadsticks (⅔ of 7-ounce can)
    Additional minced fresh cilantro (optional)

1. Preheat oven to 375°F. Spray two 1½-cup casseroles or ovenproof bowls with nonstick cooking spray.

2. Heat oil in medium skillet over medium heat. Add apple, carrot, onion and garlic. Cook and stir 3 to 4 minutes or until apple and onion are tender. Add flour, curry powder, salt, pepper and cloves. Cook and stir over medium heat 1 minute. Stir in water. Cook, stirring constantly, until liquid boils and thickens. Stir in chicken and tomatoes. Cook 3 to 4 minutes or until heated through. Stir in 2 tablespoons cilantro. Spoon into prepared casseroles.

3. Arrange 2 breadsticks over top of chicken mixture in each casserole. Sprinkle additional cilantro over tops, if desired.

4. Bake 15 to 17 minutes or until breadsticks are browned and filling is bubbly.   *Makes 2 servings*

Note: Leftover breadstick dough can be refrigerated in an airtight container and reserved for another use.

Curried Chicken Pot Pie

Impossibly Easy Salmon Pie

1 can (7½ ounces) salmon packed in water, drained and deboned
½ cup grated Parmesan cheese
¼ cup sliced green onions
1 jar (2 ounces) chopped pimientos, drained
½ cup low-fat (1%) cottage cheese
1 tablespoon lemon juice
1½ cups low-fat (1%) milk
¾ cup reduced-fat baking and pancake mix
2 whole eggs
2 egg whites *or* ¼ cup cholesterol-free egg substitute
¼ teaspoon salt
¼ teaspoon dried dill weed
¼ teaspoon paprika (optional)

1. Preheat oven to 375°F. Spray 9-inch pie plate with nonstick cooking spray. Combine salmon, Parmesan cheese, onions and pimientos in prepared pie plate; set aside.

2. Combine cottage cheese and lemon juice in blender or food processor; blend until smooth. Add milk, baking mix, whole eggs, egg whites, salt and dill. Blend 15 seconds. Pour over salmon mixture in pie plate. Sprinkle with paprika, if desired.

3. Bake 35 to 40 minutes or until lightly golden and knife inserted halfway between center and edge comes out clean. Cool 5 minutes. Cut into 8 wedges before serving. Garnish as desired.   *Makes 8 servings*

Impossibly Easy Salmon Pie

Zesty Turkey Pot Pie

1 tablespoon vegetable oil
1 small onion, finely chopped
1 jalapeño pepper,* seeded and minced
1 pound ground turkey
1 package (16 ounces) frozen mixed vegetables
½ teaspoon dried thyme leaves
½ teaspoon black pepper
2 cans (10¾ ounces each) golden mushroom soup
1 package (11 ounces) refrigerated breadsticks (12 breadsticks)

Jalapeño peppers can sting and irritate the skin; wear rubber gloves when handling peppers and do not touch eyes. Wash hands after handling.

1. Preheat oven to 350°F.

2. Heat oil in large skillet over medium heat. Add onion and jalapeño pepper; cook and stir 5 minutes or until tender. Crumble turkey into skillet; cook until no longer pink, stirring to separate.

3. Stir in vegetables, thyme and pepper. Cook 5 minutes until vegetables are thawed. Stir in soup. Cook 5 to 10 minutes or until mixture is heated through. Spoon turkey mixture into greased 13×9-inch casserole.

4. Pull and stretch breadsticks to lengthen, pressing ends together if necessary to reach across baking dish. Arrange breadsticks in lattice pattern over turkey, trimming ends. Bake 15 to 20 minutes or until breadsticks are golden brown. *Makes 6 servings*

Note: Mixture must be hot when spooned into casserole or breadsticks will be gummy on the bottom.

Zesty Turkey Pot Pie

Quick Chicken Jambalaya

8 boneless, skinless chicken thighs, cut in bite-size pieces
¼ teaspoon garlic salt
1 tablespoon vegetable oil
2½ cups 8-vegetable juice
1 bag (16 ounces) frozen pepper stir-fry mix
½ cup diced cooked ham
1 teaspoon hot pepper sauce
1¾ cups quick cooking rice, uncooked

Sprinkle garlic salt over chicken. In large nonstick skillet, place oil and heat to medium-high temperature. Add chicken and cook, stirring occasionally, 8 minutes or until chicken is lightly browned. Add vegetable juice, pepper stir-fry mix, ham, and hot pepper sauce. Heat to boiling; cover and cook over medium heat 4 minutes. Stir in rice; heat to boiling. Cover, remove pan from heat and let stand 5 minutes or until rice and vegetables are tender and liquid is absorbed. *Makes 4 servings*

Favorite recipe from **Delmarva Poultry Industry, Inc.**

❧ *Tip* ❧

Jambalaya is a Creole dish that combines rice with ham, sausage, shrimp or chicken in a tomato-based sauce containing onion, green pepper and seasonings. The name is thought to have come from the French word for ham, "jambon." Because jambalaya makes good use of leftovers, the ingredients vary widely from cook to cook.

Quick Chicken Jambalaya

Chicken Garden "Risotto"

2 boneless, skinless chicken breast halves

2 tablespoons CRISCO® Oil*

1 large sweet onion, finely chopped

1 tablespoon jarred minced garlic (or 2 large garlic cloves, peeled and minced)

1¾ cups (12 ounces) uncooked orzo pasta

2 cups broccoli flowerets, cut into bite-size pieces *or* 1 package (10½ ounces) frozen broccoli, thawed

2 cans (14½ ounces each) reduced sodium chicken stock or broth

2 ears fresh corn, kernels cut from cobs *or* 1 package (10½ ounces) frozen corn, thawed

¼ teaspoon salt

¼ teaspoon freshly ground black pepper

¾ cup freshly grated Parmesan cheese

Use your favorite Crisco Oil product.

1. Rinse chicken. Pat dry. Cut into 1-inch pieces.

2. Heat oil in 12-inch skillet on medium-high heat. Add onion and garlic. Cook 2 minutes. Add orzo, broccoli and broth. Reduce heat to medium. Cover skillet. Cook 6 minutes, stirring frequently. Add chicken. Cook 6 minutes. Mix in corn, salt and pepper. Cook 5 minutes.

3. Remove pan from heat. Stir in cheese gently. Serve hot.

Makes 4 to 6 servings

Note: Any combination of vegetables can be used, such as fresh or frozen peas, sliced carrots, sliced mushrooms, sliced zucchini or yellow squash.

Prep Time: 20 minutes
Total Time: 35 minutes

My Favorites

Favorite recipe: _____

Favorite recipe from: _____

Ingredients: _____

_____

_____

_____

_____

_____

Method: _____

_____

_____

_____

_____

_____

_____

_____

_____

_____

_____

My Favorite Recipes

Favorite recipe: _____

Favorite recipe from: _____

Ingredients: _____

_____

_____

_____

_____

_____

Method: _____

_____

_____

_____

_____

_____

_____

_____

_____

_____

_____

_____

242

Favorite recipe: _____

Favorite recipe from: _____

Ingredients: _____

_____

_____

_____

_____

_____

Method: _____

_____

_____

_____

_____

_____

_____

_____

_____

_____

_____

_____

Favorite recipe: _____

Favorite recipe from: _____

Ingredients: _____

_____

_____

_____

_____

Method: _____

_____

_____

_____

_____

_____

_____

_____

_____

_____

_____

My Favorite Recipes

Favorite recipe: _____

Favorite recipe from: _____

Ingredients: _____

_____

_____

_____

_____

_____

Method: _____

_____

_____

_____

_____

_____

_____

_____

_____

_____

_____

_____

_____

Favorite recipe: _____

Favorite recipe from: _____

Ingredients: _____

_____

_____

_____

_____

_____

Method: _____

_____

_____

_____

_____

_____

_____

_____

_____

_____

_____

_____

My Favorite Recipes

Favorite recipe: _____

Favorite recipe from: _____

Ingredients: _____

_____

_____

_____

_____

_____

Method: _____

_____

_____

_____

_____

_____

_____

_____

_____

_____

_____

_____

_____

My Favorite Recipes

Favorite recipe: _____

Favorite recipe from: _____

Ingredients: _____

_____

_____

_____

_____

_____

Method: _____

_____

_____

_____

_____

_____

_____

_____

_____

_____

_____

Favorite recipe: _____

Favorite recipe from: _____

Ingredients: _____

_____

_____

_____

_____

_____

Method: _____

_____

_____

_____

_____

_____

_____

_____

_____

_____

_____

Favorite recipe: _____

Favorite recipe from: _____

Ingredients: _____

_____

_____

_____

_____

Method: _____

_____

_____

_____

_____

_____

_____

_____

_____

_____

_____

Favorite recipe: _____

Favorite recipe from: _____

Ingredients: _____

_____

_____

_____

_____

_____

Method: _____

_____

_____

_____

_____

_____

_____

_____

_____

_____

_____

_____

Favorite recipe: _____

Favorite recipe from: _____

Ingredients: _____

_____

_____

_____

_____

Method: _____

_____

_____

_____

_____

_____

_____

_____

_____

_____

_____

My Favorite Recipes

Favorite recipe: _____

Favorite recipe from: _____

Ingredients: _____

_____

_____

_____

_____

_____

Method: _____

_____

_____

_____

_____

_____

_____

_____

_____

_____

_____

_____

Favorite recipe: _____

Favorite recipe from: _____

Ingredients: _____

_____

_____

_____

_____

_____

Method: _____

_____

_____

_____

_____

_____

_____

_____

_____

_____

_____

My Favorite Recipes

Favorite recipe: _____

Favorite recipe from: _____

Ingredients: _____

_____

_____

_____

_____

_____

Method: _____

_____

_____

_____

_____

_____

_____

_____

_____

_____

_____

_____

Favorite recipe: _____

Favorite recipe from: _____

Ingredients: _____

_____

_____

_____

_____

_____

Method: _____

_____

_____

_____

_____

_____

_____

_____

_____

_____

_____

_____

My Favorite Recipes

Favorite recipe: _____

Favorite recipe from: _____

Ingredients: _____

_____

_____

_____

_____

_____

Method: _____

_____

_____

_____

_____

_____

_____

_____

_____

_____

_____

_____

Favorite recipe: _____

Favorite recipe from: _____

Ingredients: _____

_____

_____

_____

_____

Method: _____

_____

_____

_____

_____

_____

_____

_____

_____

_____

_____

My Favorite Recipes

Favorite recipe: _____

Favorite recipe from: _____

Ingredients: _____

_____

_____

_____

_____

_____

Method: _____

_____

_____

_____

_____

_____

_____

_____

_____

_____

_____

Favorite recipe: _____

Favorite recipe from: _____

Ingredients: _____

_____

_____

_____

_____

_____

Method: _____

_____

_____

_____

_____

_____

_____

_____

_____

_____

_____

My Favorite Dinner Party

Date: _____

Occasion: _____

_____

Guests: _____

_____

_____

_____

_____

Menu: _____

_____

_____

_____

_____

_____

_____

_____

_____

_____

_____

My Favorite Dinner Party

Date: _____

Occasion: _____

_____

Guests: _____

_____

_____

_____

_____

Menu: _____

_____

_____

_____

_____

_____

_____

_____

_____

_____

_____

My Favorite Dinner Party

Date: _____

Occasion: _____

_____

Guests: _____

_____

_____

_____

_____

Menu: _____

_____

_____

_____

_____

_____

_____

_____

_____

_____

_____

_____

My Favorite Dinner Party

Date: _____

Occasion: _____

_____

Guests: _____

_____

_____

_____

Menu: _____

_____

_____

_____

_____

_____

_____

_____

_____

_____

My Favorite Dinner Party

Date: _____

Occasion: _____

_____

Guests: _____

_____

_____

_____

_____

Menu: _____

_____

_____

_____

_____

_____

_____

_____

_____

_____

_____

My Favorite Potluck

_____

Occasion: _____

_____

Guests: _____

_____

_____

_____

_____

Menu: _____

_____

_____

_____

_____

_____

_____

_____

_____

_____

_____

_____

My Favorite Potluck

Date: _____

Occasion: _____
_____

Guests: _____
_____
_____
_____
_____

Menu: _____
_____
_____
_____
_____
_____
_____
_____
_____
_____
_____
_____

My Favorite Potluck

_____

Occasion: _____

_____

Guests: _____

_____

_____

_____

Menu: _____

_____

_____

_____

_____

_____

_____

_____

_____

_____

Friend: _____

Date: _____

Food Gift: _____

_____

_____

_____

_____

_____

_____

_____

_____

_____

_____

_____

_____

_____

_____

_____

_____

_____

_____

_____

Friend: _____

Date: _____

Food Gift: _____

_____

_____

_____

_____

_____

_____

_____

_____

_____

_____

_____

_____

_____

_____

_____

_____

My Favorite Friends

Friend: _____

Favorite foods: _____

_____

_____

_____

_____

_____

Don't serve: _____

_____

_____

_____

_____

_____

_____

_____

_____

_____

_____

_____

_____

_____

My Favorite Friends

Friend: _____

Favorite foods: _____

_____

_____

_____

_____

_____

Don't serve: _____

_____

_____

_____

_____

_____

_____

_____

_____

_____

_____

_____

Hints, Tips & Index

Casserole Cookware

Casserole cookware comes in a variety of shapes, sizes and materials that fall into 2 general descriptions. They can be either deep, round containers with handles and tight-fitting lids or square and rectangular baking dishes. Casseroles are made out of glass, ceramic or metal. When making a casserole, it's important to bake the casserole in the proper size dish so that the ingredients cook evenly in the time specified.

Size Unknown?

If the size of the casserole or baking dish isn't marked on the bottom of the dish, it can be measured to determine the size.

• Round and oval casseroles are measured by volume, not inches, and are always listed by quart capacity. Fill a measuring cup with water and pour it into an empty casserole. Repeat until the casserole is filled with water, keeping track of the amount of water added. The amount of water is equivalent to the size of the dish.

• Square and rectangular baking dishes are usually measured in inches. If the dimensions aren't marked on the bottom of a square or rectangular baking dish, use a ruler to measure on top from the inside of one edge to the inside of the edge across.

Helpful Preparation Techniques

Some of the recipes call for advance preparations, such as cooked chicken or pasta. In order to ensure success when following and preparing the recipes, here are several preparation tips and techniques.

• Tips for Cooking Pasta

For every pound of pasta, bring 4 to 6 quarts of water to a full, rolling boil. Gradually add pasta, allowing water to return to a boil. Stir frequently to prevent the pasta from sticking together.

Pasta is finished cooking when it is tender but still firm to the bite, or al dente. The pasta continues to cook when the casserole is placed in the

273

oven so it is important that the pasta be slightly undercooked. Otherwise, the more the pasta cooks, the softer it becomes and, eventually, it will fall apart.

Immediately drain pasta to prevent overcooking. For best results, combine pasta with other ingredients immediately after draining.

• Tips for Cooking Rice
The different types of rice require different amounts of water and cooking times. Follow the package instructions for the best results.

Measure the amount of water specified on the package and pour into a medium saucepan. Bring to a boil over medium-high heat. Slowly add rice and return to a boil. Reduce heat to low. Cover and simmer for the time specified on the package or until the rice is tender and most of the water has been absorbed.

To test the rice for doneness, bite into a grain or squeeze a grain between your thumb and index finger. The rice is done when it is tender and the center is not hard.

• Tips for Chopping and Storing Fresh Herbs
To chop fresh herbs, place in glass measuring cup. Snip herbs into small pieces with kitchen scissors.

Wrap remaining fresh herbs in a slightly damp paper towel and place in an airtight plastic food storage bag. Store up to 5 days in the refrigerator.

Top it Off!
Buttery, golden brown bread crumbs are a popular choice when it comes to topping a casserole but the selections shouldn't end there. Be creative with the many choices available to jazz up an old favorite or just vary how they are used. Crispy toppings can be crushed, partially crushed, broken into bite-size pieces or left whole. Fruits, vegetables and other toppings

can be chopped, sliced or shredded. Sprinkle a new spice or herb in place of another one. All the toppings can be placed on top of the casserole in a variety of ways–a small amount in the center, around the edges as a border or in straight or diagonal lines across the top.

Crispy toppings add a nice texture to your casseroles. Choose from crushed unsweetened cereals; potato, corn, tortilla or bagel chips; pretzels; flour or corn tortilla strips; plain or flavored croutons; flavored crackers; crumbled bacon; ramen or chow mein noodles; sesame seeds; French fried onions and various nuts. As a guide, add 1 tablespoon melted margarine to ½ cup crushed crumbs. Sprinkle over casserole and bake to add buttery flavor.

Fruits, vegetables and other toppings add a burst of color to most casseroles. Add green, red or white onions; orange or lemon peel; mushrooms; dried or fresh fruits, such as apples, apricots, cranberries, dates, oranges, pineapple and raisins; olives; bell or chili peppers; bean sprouts; tomatoes; avocados; celery; corn; coconut; carrots; fresh herbs and shredded cheeses according to what flavor and look you desire. In order to keep the fruits and vegetables bright and crisp, add them 5 minutes before the casserole is finished cooking or sprinkle them on after it's out of the oven.

• Homemade Bread Crumbs

Making your own bread crumbs is a great way to use up the rest of a fresh loaf. To make bread crumbs, preheat oven to 300°F. Place a single layer of bread slices on a baking sheet and bake 5 to 8 minutes or until completely dry and lightly browned. Cool completely. Process in food processor or crumble in resealable plastic food storage bag until very fine. For additional flavor, season with salt, pepper and a small amount of dried herbs, ground spices or grated cheese as desired. Generally, 1 slice of bread equals ⅓ cup bread crumbs.

The Basics

• As with conventional cooking recipes, slow cooker recipe time ranges are provided to account for variables such as temperature of ingredients before cooking, how full the slow cooker is and even altitude. Once you become familiar with your slow cooker you'll have a good idea which end of the time range to use.

• Manufacturers recommend that slow cookers should be one-half to three-quarters full for best results.

• Keep a lid on it! The slow cooker can take as long as twenty minutes to regain the heat lost when the cover is removed. If the recipe calls for stirring or checking the dish near the end of the cooking time, replace the lid as quickly as you can.

• To clean your slow cooker, follow the manufacturer's instructions. To make cleanup even easier, spray with nonstick cooking spray before adding food.

• Always taste the finished dish before serving and adjust seasonings to your preference. Consider adding a dash of any of the following: salt, pepper, seasoned salt, seasoned herb blends, lemon juice, soy sauce, Worcestershire sauce, flavored vinegar, freshly ground pepper or minced fresh herbs.

TIPS & TECHNIQUES

Adapting Recipes

If you'd like to adapt your own favorite recipe to a slow cooker, you'll need to follow a few guidelines. First, try to find a similar recipe in this publication or your manufacturer's guide. Note the cooking times, liquid, quantity and size of meat and vegetable pieces. Because the slow cooker captures moisture, you will want to reduce the amount of liquid, often by as much as half. Add dairy products toward the end of the cooking time so they do not curdle.

Selecting the Right Meat

A good tip to keep in mind while shopping is that you can, and in fact should, use tougher, inexpensive cuts of meat. Top-quality cuts, such as loin chops or filet mignon, fall apart during long cooking periods. Keep those for roasting, broiling or grilling and save money when you use your slow cooker. You will be amazed to find even the toughest cuts come out fork-tender and flavorful.

Reducing Fat

The slow cooker can help you make meals lower in fat because you won't be cooking in fat as you do when you stir-fry and sauté. And tougher cuts of meat have less fat than prime cuts.

If you do use fatty cuts, such as ribs, consider browning them first on top of the range to cook off excess fat.

Chicken skin tends to shrivel and curl in the slow cooker; therefore, most recipes call for skinless chicken. If you use skin-on pieces, brown them before adding them to the slow cooker. If you would rather remove the skin, use the folowing technique: Freeze chicken until firm, but not hard. (Do not refreeze thawed chicken.) Grasp skin with clean cotton kitchen towel or paper towel and pull away from meat; discard skin. When finished skinning chicken, launder towel before using again.

You can easily remove most of the fat from accumulated juices, soups and canned broths. The simplest way is to refrigerate the liquid for several hours or overnight. The fat will congeal and float to the top for easy removal. If you plan to use the liquid right away, ladle it into a bowl or measuring cup. Let it stand about 5 minutes so the fat can rise to the surface. Skim with a large spoon. You can also lightly pull a sheet of clean paper towel over the surface, letting the grease be absorbed. To degrease canned broth, refrigerate the unopened can. Simply spoon the congealed fat off the surface after opening the can.

277

Cutting Your Vegetables

Vegetables often take longer to cook than meats. Cut vegetables into small, thin pieces and place them on the bottom or near the sides of the slow cooker. Pay careful attention to the recipe instructions in order to cut vegetables to the proper size.

Foil to the Rescue

To easily lift a dish or a meat loaf out of the slow cooker, make foil handles according to the following directions.

• Tear off three 18×3-inch strips of heavy-duty foil. Crisscross the strips so they resemble the spokes of a wheel. Place your dish or food in the center of the strips.

• Pull the foil strips up and place into the slow cooker. Leave them in while you cook so you can easily lift the item out again when ready.

Food Safety Tips

If you do any advance preparation, such as trimming meat or cutting vegetables, make sure you keep the food covered and refrigerated until you're ready to start cooking. Store uncooked meats and vegetables separately. If you are preparing meat, poultry or fish, remember to wash your cutting board, utensils and hands before touching other foods.

Once your dish is cooked, don't keep it in the slow cooker too long. Foods need to be kept cooler than 40°F or hotter than 140°F to avoid the growth of harmful bacteria. Remove food to a clean container and cover and refrigerate as soon as possible. Do not reheat leftovers in the slow cooker. Use a microwave oven, the range-top or the oven for reheating.

How Much of This=That

How much of this equals that?

Beans	1 cup = 6½ ounces 1 pound = 2½ cups 1 (8-ounce) package = 2¼ cups
Cheese	1 cup shredded = 4 ounces ¼ pound = 1 cup grated
Chicken	1 large boned breast = 2 cups cubed cooked meat
Garlic	2 medium cloves = 1 teaspoon minced
Herbs	1 tablespoon fresh = 1 teaspoon dried
Lemons	1 medium = 1 to 3 tablespoons juice and 2 to 3 teaspoons grated peel
Mushrooms	1 pound = about 6 cups sliced
Onions, yellow	1 medium = ½ to ¾ cup chopped 1 pound = about 6 cups sliced
Peppers, bell	1 large = 1 cup chopped
Rice, brown, uncooked	1 cup = 3 to 4 cups cooked
Rice, long grain uncooked	1 cup = 3 cups cooked 1 pound = 2¼ , cups, uncooked
Shrimp	1 pound = 10 to 15 jumbo 1 pound = 16 to 20 large 1 pound = 25 to 30 medium
Tomatoes	1 pound (3 medium) = 1½ cups peeled and seeded

If you don't have:	**Use:**
1 cup buttermilk	1 tablespoon lemon juice or vinegar plus milk to equal 1 cup (stir; let stand 5 minutes)
1 tablespoon cornstarch	2 tablespoons all-purpose flour or 2 teaspoons arrowroot.
1 cup beef or chicken broth	1 bouillon cube or 1 teaspoon granules mixed with 1 cup boiling water
1 small clove garlic	⅛ teaspoon garlic powder
1 tablespoon prepared mustard	1 teaspoon dry mustard
1 cup tomato sauce	½ cup tomato paste plus ½ cup cold water
1 teaspoon vinegar	2 teaspoons lemon juice
1 cup whole milk	1 cup skim milk plus 2 tablespoons melted butter
1 cup sour cream	1 cup plain yogurt

Is It Done Yet?

Use the following guides to test for doneness.

CASSEROLES
until hot and bubbly
until heated through
until cheese melts

MEAT

Beef
medium   140°F to 145°F
well done 160°F

Veal
medium   145°F to 150°F
well done 160°F

Lamb
medium   145°F
well done 160°F

Pork
well done 165°F to 170°F

POULTRY

Chicken
until temperature in thigh
    is 180°F (whole bird)
until chicken is no longer
    pink in center
until temperature in breast
    is 170°F

SEAFOOD

Fish
until fish begins to flake
    against the grain when
    tested with fork

Shrimp
until shrimp are pink and
    opaque

SAUCES
until (slightly) thickened

SOUPS
until heated through

STEWS
until meat is tender
until vegetables are tender

VEGETABLES
until crisp-tender
until tender
until browned

Metric Conversion Chart

VOLUME MEASUREMENTS (dry)

1/8 teaspoon = 0.5 mL
1/4 teaspoon = 1 mL
1/2 teaspoon = 2 mL
3/4 teaspoon = 4 mL
1 teaspoon = 5 mL
1 tablespoon = 15 mL
2 tablespoons = 30 mL
1/4 cup = 60 mL
1/3 cup = 75 mL
1/2 cup = 125 mL
2/3 cup = 150 mL
3/4 cup = 175 mL
1 cup = 250 mL
2 cups = 1 pint = 500 mL
3 cups = 750 mL
4 cups = 1 quart = 1 L

VOLUME MEASUREMENTS (fluid)

1 fluid ounce (2 tablespoons) = 30 mL
4 fluid ounces (1/2 cup) = 125 mL
8 fluid ounces (1 cup) = 250 mL
12 fluid ounces (1 1/2 cups) = 375 mL
16 fluid ounces (2 cups) = 500 mL

WEIGHTS (mass)

1/2 ounce = 15 g
1 ounce = 30 g
3 ounces = 90 g
4 ounces = 120 g
8 ounces = 225 g
10 ounces = 285 g
12 ounces = 360 g
16 ounces = 1 pound = 450 g

DIMENSIONS

1/16 inch = 2 mm
1/8 inch = 3 mm
1/4 inch = 6 mm
1/2 inch = 1.5 cm
3/4 inch = 2 cm
1 inch = 2.5 cm

OVEN TEMPERATURES

250°F = 120°C
275°F = 140°C
300°F = 150°C
325°F = 160°C
350°F = 180°C
375°F = 190°C
400°F = 200°C
425°F = 220°C
450°F = 230°C

BAKING PAN SIZES

Utensil	Size in Inches/Quarts	Metric Volume	Size in Centimeters
Baking or Cake Pan (square or rectangular)	8×8×2	2 L	20×20×5
	9×9×2	2.5 L	23×23×5
	12×8×2	3 L	30×20×5
	13×9×2	3.5 L	33×23×5
Loaf Pan	8×4×3	1.5 L	20×10×7
	9×5×3	2 L	23×13×7
Round Layer Cake Pan	8×1½	1.2 L	20×4
	9×1½	1.5 L	23×4
Pie Plate	8×1¼	750 mL	20×3
	9×1¼	1 L	23×3
Baking Dish or Casserole	1 quart	1 L	—
	1½ quart	1.5 L	—
	2 quart	2 L	—

Acknowledgments

*The publisher would like to thank the companies and organizations
listed below for the use of their recipes and photographs
in this publication.*

American Italian Pasta Company & Makers of Mueller's®, Golden Grain
Mission®, R&F®, Martha Gooch®, Ronco®, Anthony's®, Luxury Pasta® and
Pennsylvania Dutch Noodles®

Birds Eye® Foods

Delmarva Poultry Industry, Inc.

Del Monte Corporation

The Golden Grain Company®

The Hidden Valley® Food Products Company

Hormel Foods, LLC

Jennie-O Turkey Store®

Lawry's® Foods

MASTERFOODS USA

Mrs. Dash®

National Pork Board

Perdue Farms Incorporated

Reckitt Benckiser Inc.

Crisco is a registered trademark of the J.M. Smucker Company

Unilever Foods North America

Index

Index

Index

Index

Index